GET YOUR
HOPES UP!

GET YOUR HOPES UP!

Expect Something Good to
Happen to You Every Day

. . . .

JOYCE MEYER

NEW YORK   BOSTON   NASHVILLE

Unless otherwise noted Scriptures are taken from The Amplified Bible (AMP). The Amplified Bible, Old Testament, copyright © 1965, 1987 by The Zondervan Corporation. The Amplified New Testament, copyright © 1954, 1958, 1987 by The Lockman Foundation. Used by permission.

Scriptures noted (NIV) are taken from the Holy Bible: New International Version ®. Copyright © 1973, 1978, 1984 by International Bible Society. Used by permission of Zondervan Publishing House. All rights reserved.

Scripture quotations marked (NLT) are taken from the Holy Bible, New Living Translation, Copyright © 1996. Used by permission of Tyndale House Publishers, Inc., Wheaton, Illinois 60189. All rights reserved.

FaithWords

Hachette Book Group

1290 Avenue of the Americas

New York, NY 10104

www.faithwords.com

Printed in the United States of America

RRD-H

First Edition: April 2015

10 9 8 7 6 5 4 3 2 1

FaithWords is a division of Hachette Book Group, Inc.

The FaithWords name and logo are trademarks of Hachette Book Group, Inc.

The Hachette Speakers Bureau provides a wide range of authors for speaking events. To find out more, go to www.hachettespeakersbureau.com or call (866) 376-6591.

The publisher is not responsible for websites (or their content) that are not owned by the publisher.

Library of Congress Cataloging-in-Publication Data

Meyer, Joyce, 1943-
  Get your hopes up! : expect something good to happen to you every day / Joyce Meyer. — First Edition.
      pages cm
  Includes bibliographical references.
  ISBN 978-1-4555-1731-2 (hardcover) — ISBN 978-1-4555-8951-7 (large-print hardcover) — ISBN 978-1-4555-1730-5 (ebook) — ISBN 978-1-61113-259-5 (audiobook) — ISBN 978-1-4555-3230-8 (audio download) — ISBN 978-1-4555-3231-5 (spanish trade pbk.) — ISBN 978-1-4555-8871-8 (international edition)
  1. Expectation (Psychology)—Religious aspects—Christianity.   2. Hope—Religious aspects—Christianity.   I. Title.
  BV4647.E93M49 2015
  248.4—dc23
                                                                    2014048830

And now, Lord, what do I wait for and expect? My hope and expectation are in You.

Psalm 39:7

CONTENTS

INTRODUCTION   ix

SECTION I
HOPE TO GO HIGHER

CHAPTER 1:   Raise Your Level of Expectation   3

CHAPTER 2:   Follow the Leader   14

CHAPTER 3:   Identify and Eliminate Every "Can't"   24

CHAPTER 4:   The Energy of Hope   34

CHAPTER 5:   Getting to Know the New You   45

SECTION II
HOPE WHEN YOU'RE HURTING

CHAPTER 6:   Look Up   57

CHAPTER 7:   Count Your Blessings Instead of Your Problems   66

CHAPTER 8:   Words of Hope   76

CHAPTER 9:   Keep Moving   86

SECTION III
HOPE AND HAPPINESS

CHAPTER 10: Look for the Good in Everything   99

CHAPTER 11: Prisoners of Hope   109

CHAPTER 12: Be an Answer to Someone's Prayer   118

CHAPTER 13: Hope Is Our Anchor   128

SECTION IV
HOPE IS HERE

CHAPTER 14: Don't Wait for Tomorrow   139

CHAPTER 15: Get God's Perspective   146

CHAPTER 16: The Choice Is Yours   156

CHAPTER 17: Let Hope Overflow   166

AFTERWORD   177

NOTES   179

ADDITIONAL BIBLE VERSES ABOUT HOPE   181

Without faith, it is impossible to please God, and those who come to Him must believe that He is a Rewarder of those who diligently seek Him (see Hebrews 11:6). Faith is the title deed of the things we *hope* for (see Hebrews 11:1). We are promised in God's Word that faith the size of a mustard seed can move a mountain (see Matthew 17:20). Abraham *hoped* in faith that he would receive the promise of God (see Romans 4:18). Some people try to have faith, but they have no hope. They don't have a positive expectation that something good is going to happen to them because of God's great goodness. I believe hope precedes and is connected with faith. We cannot have one without the other. How could a negative, hopeless person be walking and living by faith? The person may believe in God, but a man or woman of faith does more than trust that God is alive; they also believe that He is good, and that He rewards those who seek Him. They wait for and expect the goodness of God, not because they deserve it, but because God promises to give it.

I've spent the last 38 years of my life traveling the world, preaching and teaching the Word of God. Over that time, I've met so many incredible people—people just like you. Business owners, housewives, working moms, artists, ministers, entrepreneurs, politicians, volunteers, single moms, single dads. I've had the privilege of meeting men and women from nearly every walk of life.

Some are doing great, seemingly on top of the world. Others have confided to me that they're barely getting by, living day to day, trying to make ends meet. And many others are dealing with circumstances so difficult that, quite frankly, they feel defeated and overwhelmed by life.

But no matter the person, and no matter the situation, I've discovered there is one thing they all desperately need—one thing we *all* desperately need: hope.

Hope is the happy and confident anticipation of good. It's a powerful and universal inspiration, a rising tide that lifts all boats. Whether we are limping into port, stuck at the dock, or sailing boldly out to sea, hope buoys our spirits, daring us to believe *You know what? Things might just work out after all.* It's the sometimes unexplainable, but always undeniable, feeling that today would be a bad day to give up. Hope is a belief that something good is about to happen at any moment!

This is why I believe a book on hope is necessary and that it will help you see hope's amazing possibilities. In fact, the Bible tells us it is one of the three things that remain when all else fails (see 1 Corinthians 13:13). Regardless of who you are or what condition your life is in right now, you can't function successfully in life without hope. If circumstances are bad, you surely need hope, and if they are good, you need hope that they will stay that way. When you live in the garden of hope, something is always blooming!

But as great as hope is, it can easily be misplaced. If your hope clings to a person, it's an unreliable source of strength. If your hope is in your place of employment, your ability to make money, or your retirement fund, it may disappoint you. If your hope rests in your own ability, it will fade when your confidence is shaken.

It's pretty simple, really: Hope is only as strong as its source. That's why the foundation of our hope must be God and the promises found in His Word. If God is not the source, hope is just a wishful thought, a momentary respite. As a matter of fact, the hope I am urging you to have is very different from what the world might call hope. The believer's hope is in the unshakable, all-powerful, all-knowing, and ever-present one true God and His Son, Jesus Christ.

You could say it this way: Without hope in God, there isn't much you can do, but *with* hope in God, there isn't much you *can't* do.

Dedicated reading and study of the Word shows us what happens when God's children dared to live with hope. Throughout the Old and New Testament, we see regular people—people with flaws and failures just like us—overcome impossible odds because they chose to hope that God had something incredible on the horizon...they put their faith in Him.

• Though the Hebrew children had been slaves in Egypt for many generations, the hope of freedom compelled Moses to dream of deliverance from their cruel oppressors.

• While the Israelite army hid in the trenches in fear of Goliath, the hope for victory caused David to ask "What shall be done for the man who kills this Philistine and takes away the reproach from Israel?" (1 Samuel 17:26).

• In the face of Haman's evil plot to destroy her people, the hope that she could make a difference gave Esther the courage to break convention and request an audience with the king.

• Leaving jobs, friends, and even family behind, the hope that Jesus could be the promised Messiah caused ordinary men to drop everything and follow Him all the way to the cross.

Do you see the wide-ranging, barrier-shattering nature of hope? In each of these biblical examples, hope was more than a motivational thought or a fading daydream; hope was a *nothing-is-impossible-with-God* firestorm refusing to be quenched.

• For Moses, hope broke chains.
• For David, hope asked the question no one else had the courage to ask.

- For Esther, hope believed against all odds that God could use her to save her people from destruction.
- For the disciples, hope gave them courage to embark on a new life and become world changers.

I believe hope can do those same things in your life. That's why I'm excited you're reading this book. And that's why I'm excited to use the stories, biblical principles, and practical life lessons you'll find on each page to encourage you to go ahead and *get your hopes up!* Do it on purpose...grab hold passionately and refuse to live without hope!

You see, your whole life, whether you realize it or not, the world has been telling you *Don't get your hopes up.* Past hurts, present disappointments, and future uncertainties all teach you to temper your expectations—*Be rational, stay calm, don't expect too much because you may get disappointed.*

The pregnancy test comes back positive... *don't get your hopes up; you remember what happened last time.* The person who hurt you apologizes and wants to make things right... *don't get your hopes up; he might hurt you again.* An exciting opportunity opens up at work... *don't get your hopes up; it probably won't pan out.*

But a life with no hope isn't much of a life at all. You may say you're just being careful—*Better safe than sorry, Joyce*—but you're really just afraid. Afraid of getting hurt, afraid of being disappointed, afraid of taking a chance. The fear may exist for good reason. Perhaps you have been severely hurt in life and experienced many discouraging and disappointing things. Experience tells you that nothing is ever going to change, but God's Word tells us something better. It says that all things are possible with God!

It is time for a change in your life! Trust God enough to hope for the best: the best relationship, the best opportunity, the best marriage, the best news, the best outcome, the best life. Expect something good to happen to you today!

God wants you to have the best life possible. If you ever doubt that's true, just remember that He gave His best when He sent Jesus. Jesus died so that, if you accept His gift of salvation, you could enjoy eternity in Heaven; but He also died so you could enjoy a good life here on Earth.

In John 10:10, Jesus said, "I came that they may have and enjoy life, and have it in abundance (to the full, till it overflows)."

As you go through this book, I hope you'll see that God wants you to "have and enjoy life." He wants the best for you spiritually, mentally, emotionally, relationally, and physically—every year, every day, every moment. And when you know that God wants the best for you, you can't help but be filled with hope. God wants to meet all your needs and enable you to help other people.

> So, if you're hurting today, doubting if things will ever get better... *get your hopes up.*
>
> If you're just getting by in life, going through the motions but asking if there is anything more... *get your hopes up.*
>
> If you're raising children, wondering what life has in store for them... *get your hopes up.*
>
> If you're starting out on an exciting new adventure, risking more than you've ever risked before... *get your hopes up.*

When you dare to get your hopes up, things will begin to change in your life. Faith increases, joy returns, and peace reigns. So if you're satisfied to settle for *barely getting by, this is as good as it gets,* or *better luck next time,* you should probably put this book down now.

But if you're ready for a change—if you're ready for something better—keep reading. Hope has a way of beautifully transforming the lives of all who embrace it. It's the catalyst that sparks ideas and imagination (see Proverbs 24:14), the anchor that steadies us when the storms of life rage (see Hebrews 6:19), the confidence that dares us to build a better life (see Proverbs 23:18), and the comfort of knowing we're never alone (see Romans 5:5).

If that sounds good to you, be brave enough to do something you may not have done in a long time: Get your hopes up. You're going to be glad you did, because God is waiting to be gracious to you.

SECTION I

HOPE TO GO HIGHER

. . . .

. . . But those who hope in the Lord will renew their strength.
They will soar on wings like eagles . . .

Isaiah 40:31 (NIV)

Quite often people feel that it would be greedy or wrong to hope for more than they have. While it is true that we should always be content and satisfied with what we have, that certainly doesn't mean that desiring more of the right things is wrong as long as we desire them for the right reasons. How can we be content and yet want more at the same time? I am very content right now with everything in my life because I believe God's timing in my life is perfect. I could be quite happy and never have more of anything because my joy and contentment are in Christ. Yet, at the same time, I want more of everything because I want to go as far in life as God allows and do as much for Him and others as humanly possible. I want no more and no less than the best life God wants to give me!

I want more of God in my life, a closer, more intimate walk with Him (see Philippians 3:10). I want more wisdom, more stability, and more good friends. I want more for my children, and I want more people to accept Christ as their Savior. I want to see more miracles, healing, breakthroughs, and power.

I sincerely believe that we can be satisfied to the point where we are not disturbed or disquieted with what we have, while at the same time desiring more for the right reasons and at the right time (see Philippians 4:11, 19).

I actually believe those who are content with anything less than all God can do for them are hindering God's greatness. He wants to show Himself strong in each of our lives. He is able to do exceedingly, abundantly, above and beyond all that we could ever dare to ask or think, infinitely beyond our highest prayers, desires, thoughts, hopes, or dreams (see Ephesians 3:20).

CHAPTER 1

Raise Your Level of Expectation

*Wait and hope for and expect the Lord; be brave and of good
courage and let your heart be stout and enduring. Yes, wait
for and hope for and expect the Lord.*

Psalm 27:14

"High expectations are the key to everything."

—Sam Walton

Let me tell you a story about a woman named Betty. Betty is a
believer. She reads her Bible on a regular basis. And she volunteers
by passing out blankets to the homeless once a month. Betty sounds
beautiful, doesn't she?

Well, there is something else about Betty you should know: Her
friends call her "Bad-News Betty" when she's not around. They feel
terrible about the nickname, but in all fairness, Betty has earned
it; she has a way of expecting, predicting, and finding the worst in
almost every situation. I'll give you an example.

Last summer, Betty and her husband (Failure Phil) went on a
family vacation with their two children (Won't-Amount-to-Much
Will and Middle-of-the-Pack Megan). Now, I should tell you that
Phil is a loving husband and Will and Megan are great kids, but
Betty doesn't have high hopes for them. She doesn't expect much
for them either. As a matter of fact, she kind of assumes the worst,
hence their nicknames.

Months earlier, Phil and Betty had planned a summer week at a popular vacation destination, but as the trip grew closer, Betty just knew it was going to be a disaster. As they drove the 300 miles to their vacation spot, Betty kept complaining, "This was a bad idea. The lines to do anything in the park are going to be a mile long. I doubt the hotel will be as good as advertised. I bet it's going to rain the whole week." Phil and the kids tried to assure Betty it would be fine—they could make the best of any situation—but Betty's sour mood was unfazed. Poor Phil, Will, and Megan...the 300-mile drive felt like 1,000 miles of drudgery.

It's safe to say the vacation lived down to Betty's expectations. The lines at the water park were a little longer than usual. Phil, Will, and Megan didn't mind—this gave them a few extra minutes to laugh together and plan what ride to go on next—but Betty was terribly upset. "I knew this was going to happen," she muttered.

The restaurant they chose to dine at the first night wasn't perfect either. The waitress informed Phil and Betty they were out of the soft drink the couple ordered. Phil chose a different drink; Betty chose a depressing attitude. "Unbelievable!" she sighed.

But the straw that broke the camel's back was the hotel room. When the family settled into their room for the night, they discovered the TV wasn't working properly. "I knew it! I knew it! I knew it!" an exasperated Betty griped. "I knew this hotel wasn't going to be any good." Phil called the front desk, and maintenance quickly brought a new television up, but the damage was already done.

Bad-News Betty had her bad-news vacation...this was exactly what she expected.

An Issue of the Heart

The story of Betty is a fictitious account of someone who looks an awful lot like you and me at times. We've all found ourselves dealing with pessimistic attitudes and low expectations—describing the weather as "partly cloudy" rather than "partly sunny," seeing the glass as "half empty" instead of "half full."

For Betty, her low expectations kept her from enjoying a summer vacation, but for many people, low expectations keep them from enjoying their lives. They go through each day with negative, faultfinding, critical attitudes, rarely hoping for the best because they're too busy expecting the worst. When things are going poorly they think *I had a feeling today was going to be a bad day*, and when things are going well they think *This probably won't last long*. Good days or bad, on the mountaintop or in the valley, they're not enjoying their lives...because they've never expected they could. Perhaps you and I are not as bad as Betty, but to be honest, any degree of hopelessness has a devastating effect on our lives. Why not believe the best and open the door to see what God will do?

Low expectations are more than a few grumpy complaints on a longer-than-usual Monday or a feeling that maybe you woke up on the wrong side of the bed. Low expectations are symptoms of a deeper problem, a *spiritual* problem. A person may have a history of disappointments that caused him to form a habit of expecting more of the same. Some people have such low self-esteem that they assume they are not worth anything nice, so they never expect it. And then there are those who don't know that God is good and wants to do good things for His children. The risks these symptoms pose are significant. If we were to describe what's happening in our souls the same way we would describe a physical ailment, it might sound something like this:

Doctor: So, you say you're spiritually and emotionally under the weather. Please tell me your symptoms.

Patient: Well, Doctor, I've got a bad feeling about the future. I have had a lot of disappointments in my life, and I rarely expect things to work out for me or for my family.

Doctor: Your symptoms tell me everything I need to know. You've got a bad case of hopelessness.

Betty's symptoms were negativity, worry, and complaining. These symptoms were caused by a condition of her heart: hopelessness. Instead of hoping for a great family vacation, Betty assumed the worst. *The lines are going to be long. We'll never find a good restaurant. The hotel will be terrible.* There is no hope in any of those thoughts. However, Phil, Will, and Megan had different symptoms. They were positive, upbeat, cheerful, and ready to make the most of any situation. They were full of hope, and their expectations were sky high.

It's important to realize that the circumstances were the same for Betty and her family, but the ways they reacted to those circumstances were different. They all stood in long lines; they all ate at the same restaurant; they all sat down in front of the broken television. When these things happened, Betty's low expectations were confirmed, causing her to want to give up. For the rest of the family, their high expectations were challenged, but they chose to remain hopeful and joyful, which enabled them to find ways to deal with the circumstances and move on, enjoying every step of the way.

With that picture in mind, let me ask you an important question: What are your symptoms? If you were to conduct an honest evaluation of your heart, what would you find there?

Are you like Phil, Will, and Megan? Excited about the future, expecting today to be better than yesterday and tomorrow to be even better than today? Do you wake up each morning with a happy anticipation that God is going to do something amazing in your life?

> *Do you wake up each morning with a happy anticipation that God is going to do something amazing in your life?*

Or are you more like Bad-News Betty? Do you find yourself bracing for the worst? Do you worry about bad things happening before they actually happen? Do you use phrases like *here we go again, this will never work out, I should've known things would go sour,* and *I've got a bad feeling about this?*

The Faith Connection

Evaluating our hearts is an important exercise as we begin this journey of hope together, because hope in God and positive *expectation* are very closely related to faith. For the sake of discussion, we can easily say that the level of your expectation is the level of your faith. Show me a person with low expectations, and I'll show you a person using very little faith. But show me a person with big expectations, and I'll show you a person acting with bold faith. Just remember that we are talking about having our expectation in God. It

> Show me a person with big expectations, and I'll show you a person acting with bold faith.

is more than a mere positive attitude; it is trusting God to take care of you and everything that concerns you.

The Word of God tells us that our faith—our positive, hopeful expectation—pleases God (see Hebrews 11:6), and several times in the Gospels, we see that Jesus was moved to act because of the faith—the expectations—of those He encountered (see Matthew 9:29, Mark 5:34, Luke 7:50, and Luke 17:19). One such miracle is found in Mark chapter 10. I love this story, and I think it has great relevance for you and me today because it's all about the importance of expectation.

Mark 10:46–47 says:

> …As [Jesus] was leaving Jericho with His disciples and a great crowd, Bartimaeus, a blind beggar, a son of Timaeus, was sitting by the roadside. And when he heard that it was Jesus of Nazareth, he began to shout, saying, Jesus, Son of David, have pity and mercy on me [now]!

If you think about it, Bartimaeus had every reason to expect the worst. He was a blind beggar who sat by the roadside every day, trying to survive on spare change. He was living a very difficult life, and if anybody was going to tone down his level of expectation, you would think it would be Bartimaeus. He could have thought *This is useless. It won't work. Nothing's going to change. Jesus probably won't even notice me. Why get my hopes up?* No one would have blamed him.

But Bartimaeus dared to hope for something greater in life. He started to think about what might happen instead of what might not happen. There was nothing "toned down" about his level of expectation as he began to shout with all of his might, "Jesus, Son of David, have pity and mercy on me [now]!" Can you hear the insistence in his voice? It's as if Bartimaeus had decided there was absolutely no way he was going to miss this chance. Even though many in the crowd "censured and reproved him, telling him to keep still" (see Mark 10:48), Bartimaeus would not be quieted. He shouted louder and louder until Jesus stopped and called for him.

Here is one of the most amazing parts of this story: When Bartimaeus was brought to Jesus, the Lord asked him an almost unthinkable question. In verse 51, Jesus said to this blind beggar, "What do you want Me to do for you?"

That seems like a strange question, doesn't it? The disciples may have been thinking *"What do you want me to do for you?" Lord, isn't it obvious? The man is blind. How can You ask him that?* But Jesus was asking something deeper—He was asking Bartimaeus: *What are you expecting? Are you only expecting a meal? Are you wanting someone to lead you around by the hand? Are you merely expecting a handout?* All of those things were certainly things Bartimaeus needed, and if he was living with little faith, he may have settled for one of those things.

But Bartimaeus had a greater level of expectation. When Jesus asked, "What do you want Me to do for you?" Bartimaeus didn't hesitate, he didn't have to think about it, he didn't wonder if he was asking for too much. Bartimaeus boldly said, "Master, let me receive my sight." You probably know the rest of the story. Jesus was greatly moved by Bartimaeus' faith. Verse 52 says: "And Jesus said to him, Go your way; your faith has healed you. And at once he received his sight and accompanied Jesus on the road."

Because Bartimaeus was bold enough to believe for God's best, that is exactly what he received from the Lord. The same is true in your life, and this is why the level of your expectation is so important to the kind of life you're going to live. If you don't expect God to do anything great in your life, He won't. But if you dare to raise your level of expectation and begin anticipating that God wants to do something great in your life, you'll begin to dream, believe, ask, and act with a confident boldness, knowing God is for you and has a great plan for your life.

> God is for you and has a great plan for your life.

Just in case you are questioning if it is acceptable for you to expect good things from God, please slowly read and meditate on this Scripture in Isaiah.

> *And therefore the Lord [earnestly] waits [expecting, looking, and longing] to be gracious to you; and therefore He lifts Himself up, that He may have mercy on you and show loving-kindness to you. For the Lord is a God of justice. Blessed (happy, fortunate, to be envied) are all those who [earnestly] wait for Him, who expect and look and long for Him [for His victory, His favor, His love, His peace, His joy, and His matchless, unbroken companionship]!*
>
> Isaiah 30:18

God is looking for those He can be good to, and if you are looking for (expecting) God to be good to you, then you qualify. Expect God to give you Himself because He is more important than anything else, but remember that with Him comes all the other things we will ever need.

Three Steps to Raise the Level of Your Expectation

You may be reading this chapter and thinking *Joyce, that sounds great, but how am I supposed to expect more? I'm running from one appointment to another, barely paying my bills, just trying to keep the kids fed or the company afloat. And I've spent my whole life working as hard as I can to get to* this *point. How in the world do I raise my level of expectation?*

There is so much I could say about faith—thousands upon thousands of books have been written on the topic—but I want to give you three simple steps that can get you started today. These three steps will help you raise your level of expectation:

1. Believe.

   Children of God are called "believers" for a reason. When you're tempted to doubt, tempted to give up, tempted to call it quits, choose to believe instead.

   > When you're tempted to doubt, tempted to give up, tempted to call it quits, choose to believe instead.

   Belief is the basis of your faith. Believe God's Word. Believe His promises are true. Believe He loves you, and believe He has something beautiful in store for your life. Jesus said that if we would only believe, then we would see God's glory (see John 11:40). Glory is the manifestation of all of the excellence of God.

2. Ask.

   James 4:2 says: "You do not have, because you do not ask." Once you have chosen to believe God can meet every need in your life, go ahead and ask God to meet those needs. Share your dreams with Him. Just as Jesus asked Bartimaeus, "What do you want Me to do for you?" He is asking you the same question. Be bold enough to ask the Lord to do something only He can do. Obviously, we should all want God's will and trust that if what we are asking for isn't right for us, God won't give it to us but instead He will give us something better.

3. Look.

As you go through each day, expect that God is answering your prayer, meeting your need, and fulfilling your God-given dream. Even if you haven't seen the manifestation of what you desire yet, or if it has not happened in the way you hoped it would, that doesn't mean God isn't working. Continue to have an expectant attitude, and be sure to notice everything God is doing. Be thankful for those things while you are waiting for the thing you desire or need now.

Whatever you're hoping for today—a deeper walk with God, a better understanding of God's Word, a stronger marriage, a financial breakthrough, a chance to go back to school, a ministry opportunity, a fresh start—if it's in your heart (and if it lines up with the Word of God), believe, ask, expect, and look.

The Real Change that Comes with Higher Expectations

Your life will go only as high as the level of your expectations. It's not that your expectations immediately change the environment or the circumstances around you, but your expectations change the way you react to that environment and those circumstances.

> *Your life will go only as high as the level of your expectations.*

Your expectations change *you*. They cause you to be able to wait for a change in your circumstances with a happy attitude. They cause you to be a bold, confident, joy-filled believer who trusts that God has a great plan for your life.

Here's a simple story I came across that demonstrates the joy that comes with great expectations:

> There were once identical twins. They were alike in every way but one. One was a hope-filled optimist who only saw the bright side of life in every situation. The other was a dark pessimist who only saw the downside of every situation.
>
> The parents were so worried about the extremes of optimism and pessimism in their boys that they took them to the doctor. The doctor suggested a plan. "On their next birthday," he said, "give the pessimist a shiny new bike, but give the optimist only a pile of manure."
>
> It seemed a fairly extreme thing to do. After all, the parents had always treated their boys equally. But in this instance they decided to try the doctor's advice. So when the twins' birthday came around, the parents gave the pessimist the most expensive, top-of-the-line racing bike a child has ever owned. When he saw the bike, his first words were "I'll probably crash and break my leg."
>
> To the optimist, they gave a carefully wrapped box of manure. He opened it, looked puzzled for a moment, then ran outside screaming "You can't fool me! Where there's this much manure, there's gotta be a pony around here somewhere!"[1]

Get Your Hopes Up!

I want to encourage you to raise your level of expectation today. It doesn't matter what the situation looks like around you; God is greater than any obstacle you may be facing. Don't assume that where you've been, or where you are, is as good as it gets. Don't believe that your history is your destiny. Choose, instead, to believe God is going to do something even better in your life. Jesus is asking "What do you want Me to do for you?" That's a pretty powerful question, so go ahead and get your hopes up. There must be a pony around here somewhere!

> *Don't assume that where you've been, or where you are, is as good as it gets.*

CHAPTER 2

Follow the Leader

My whole being follows hard after You and clings closely to
*   You;*
Your right hand upholds me.

Psalm 63:8

"Hope is the word which God has written on the brow
of every man."

—Victor Hugo, *Les Misérables*

Of all the timeless games children play, follow the leader is perhaps
the most common. Whether it's in preschool, elementary school, or
just playing with friends at the park, at some point in time, every
child has joined a line of peers and gone about the playful task of
following the leader. Do you remember playing? Do you remember
the challenge of walking in the footsteps of the person in front of
you, even as they walked in the footsteps of the person in front of
them? Through the tunnel, across the monkey bars, up the ladder,
down the slide: All around the playground you went.

One of the things I remember most about follow the leader is
that the enjoyment of the game was directly linked to the ability
of the leader. If we had a leader with little speed, no creativity,
or a poor sense of direction, the game fell apart quickly—kids
would lose interest and go find something else to play. Similarly,

if we had a leader who was too fast, overly acrobatic, or bossy and demanding, the game wouldn't last very long because no one could keep up. In order for the game to be a success, we had to have the right leader—a leader who moved at the perfect pace, kept things interesting, and took us somewhere we wanted to go.

Leadership is key. This is a truth that is reinforced all through childhood, into adolescence, and even as we enter the "adult world." If you had a knowledgeable coach, you probably had a pretty successful team. If you were fortunate enough to get a motivated and inspiring teacher, you probably learned more about a particular subject than you would have otherwise. If your boss challenged you to be your best and put you in a position to succeed, you probably enjoyed your job and performed well at the tasks assigned to you. How much you enjoy an experience, and the level of success you achieve, is directly linked to whom you choose to follow.

What is true on the playground, at the ball field, in the classroom, and around the conference room table is true in the deeper areas of your life as well—leadership is still key. Who or what you choose to follow will determine how much you enjoy your life. But I'm not talking about following a boss, a teacher, or a parent; I'm talking about a bigger decision: the choice to follow God and His plan for your life.

If you go through life with your own agenda—trying to figure everything out, trying to follow your own plan—chances are you're going to be miserable and unhappy. It's not that your plan is inherently bad; it's just that God's plan is immeasurably better.

> *It's not that your plan is inherently bad; it's just that God's plan is immeasurably better.*

Anytime you settle for your plan instead of submitting to God's plan, you are settling for second best. Also, a great deal of stress comes with trying to force your own plan to work. As soon as you run into an obstacle—the school denies your application, a business endeavor fails, the person you hoped to marry rejects you, the house doesn't sell—the pressure builds because you feel you have to fix the problem in your own strength. If you're the leader, it's easy to lose hope, because you're well aware of your own flaws, failures, and limitations.

But if you want to live a life full of hope, the best thing you can do is turn the leadership role over to God. Let Him be the leader, and decide to follow Him wholeheartedly, trusting that He has a great plan and He is working that plan to perfection. Stop reading for a few minutes and ask yourself: *Am I aggressively following God, or am I asking God to follow me?* In God, you find a leader who moves at the perfect pace and keeps things interesting, and although He may take you a few places you'd rather not go, you will miraculously end up in the right place at the right time. Waiting on God doesn't mean you sit around and do nothing. In fact, quite the opposite is true. You still plan for the future, and you still work diligently to succeed at the tasks in front of you, but you do those things after you have spent time with God, asking for His guidance and direction. And when you do make plans, you hold on to those plans loosely. You go through each day with an attitude that says *Lord, I trust that You have a plan for my life. Point me in the direction You want me to go. Close any doors that are not part of Your plan, and open every door of opportunity You want me to enter. Lead and guide me today and every day.*

When things go wrong and circumstances get tough, people who are following God's lead don't panic. They believe that He will use any and every situation—good or bad—to bring about His plan and purposes. We all make mistakes and we learn a lot of lessons, but if we stay filled with hope, we can enjoy the journey. We may make a few detours that we were not planning for, but God's purposes will win out in the end.

Trusting God, Not Yourself

It's easier to have high hopes for your spiritual growth, your marriage, your health, your children, your relationships, your job, and your finances when you've made God the leader and you trust that He has a great plan for your life. Believing that God has a purpose for your life, and choosing to follow His guidance to see that purpose fulfilled, is a total exercise in trust.

It's a lot like the "trust fall" you've probably seen people demonstrate at one time or another. In the trust fall, one person allows himself to be vulnerable, falling backward with no net to catch him and no padding to break his fall, while another person stands behind him promising to catch him before he hits the ground. When you say, "Lord, I choose to follow Your lead. I believe Your plan is infinitely better than my plan could ever be," it's a lot like trusting someone will catch you. But there is a major difference: God does more than just catch you; God catches you and then takes you higher than you were before.

> God does more than just catch you; God catches you and then takes you higher than you were before.

Learning to trust God completely is something I've had to learn over time and am still learning daily. I used to have a habit of trusting only myself. I formed this habit after years of trying to trust people, only to end up disappointed and hurt. I would then decide to never trust anyone again. These painful experiences caused me to believe *If you want something done right, you've got to do it yourself. If you don't ask anybody for anything or open your heart to them, they can't hurt you.* But this mind-set was unhealthy, and it did more than keep me from trusting people—it kept me from trusting God. It was a bad habit I needed the Lord's help to break.

The Word of God is very clear about trusting the Lord rather than trusting in ourselves. Proverbs 3:5–6 say:

> Lean on, trust in, and be confident in the Lord with all your heart and mind and do not rely on your own insight or understanding. In all your ways know, recognize, and acknowledge Him, and He will direct and make straight and plain your paths.

To "trust in" God is simply to believe that He loves you, He's good, He has the power to help you, He wants to help you, and He *will* help you. Many times we trust everyone *except* God, or we trust everyone *before* we trust God. We trust our friends, the bank, the stock market, the government, or our own talents and abilities more than we trust God and His Word. Did you ever hear anyone say "I've done everything I know to do, but none of it is working; I guess there is nothing I can do now but pray"? Most of us have said that, and it is a revealing statement. It is another way of saying "I've tried to help myself and failed, I've tried other people and they failed, nothing I do is working, so I guess I have no recourse but to try to trust God!"

> God wants us to put Him first in our lives. He wants us to put our confidence and trust in Him…all the time…in everything.

Prayer should be our first line of defense in any battle, never a last-ditch effort after all else has failed.

God wants us to put Him first in our lives. He wants us to put our confidence and trust in Him…all the time…in everything.

He wants us to hope in Him, to have faith in Him, because when we do, we will not live disappointed, fruitless lives. He will lead us into the overcoming, abundant, joy-filled life Jesus died to give us. Remember the great song that says "My hope is built on nothing less but Jesus Christ, my righteousness"? Put all your hope in God and get ready for the most exciting journey you can imagine.

How to Follow God's Leading

If you have decided to follow the Leader (Jesus), Romans 8:1 says that, as believers, we can "live [and] walk not after the dictates of the flesh, but after the dictates of the Spirit." One of the ways you can tell if you are following the flesh (your own plan) instead of the Spirit (God's plan) is that you have no peace and you're struggling. If you're thinking about doing something but you have no peace about it, just don't do it.

For example: You may be looking for a job, but the only offer you've been given in your field of expertise is across the country. But if you haven't prayed about it, and you're making this decision without consulting God, convincing yourself you've got to move across the country because this could be your only job offer, you might be setting yourself up for years of misery. If your entire family doesn't want to go and your decision to go is causing strife and turmoil, you should wait and seek God for more clear direction.

Here's the thing: If your mind is troubled and you have no peace, and your decision is causing trouble, don't do it! Very often we try to talk ourselves into something we don't have any peace about, and that is an open invitation to trouble. In the example above, the reasoning would go something like this: "Well, I really don't want to move and my family is against it, and the job isn't what I was looking for, but it might be okay. It's the best offer I've had. I'm getting tired of waiting." Beware of this sort of reasoning, and no matter how impatient you feel, if you don't have peace about the move, you're better off waiting until God brings a better opportunity your way.

I realize you need to financially support yourself and your family, but you would be better off to take any kind of job locally while waiting for the perfect job than to make a cross-country move you have no peace about. Let peace be the umpire in your life, deciding with finality every question that arises in your mind (see Colossians 3:15).

Whatever the situation is, the same principle remains true. Whether it's finding a spouse, choosing a church, deciding on a purchase, establishing healthy boundaries in relationships, the list could go on. Always make it your goal to follow the wisdom and peace of God.

When you're not sure what decision to make—when you're not positive if you're following your own desires or God's direction— look to the umpire. Let peace make the call!

> When you're not sure what decision to make—when you're not positive if you're following your own desires or God's direction—look to the umpire. Let peace make the call!

Even when you've decided to follow God's leading in your life, there are going to be times when you make mistakes. Don't be discouraged when that happens; it is all part of learning! The disciples made mistakes when they were following Jesus. You don't ever have to be ashamed to back out of doing something you thought was God once you realize it's not. You can simply say, "I've made a mistake," and move on. I've missed God's perfect plan plenty of times, and you will too. Actually, that's one of the ways we learn how to hear from God correctly. Sometimes you will need to step out and try something to find out whether or not it's really God. If you have done all you can to discover God's will in your situation and you have no clear direction, then do what is in your heart and trust that God will lead you as you go. I often say that nobody can drive a parked car, not even God. If we have our lives in park, we may need to put them in drive and at least make a move in some direction. We often only find out as we step out!

God Is with You and He Is Leading You Every Step of the Way

It's so good to know that, as believers, we are never alone. Let me make that more personal: *You* are never alone. God doesn't lead you from some great distance away; He is living in your heart and walking with you step by step, no matter what you go through. Though it may look like there is no one standing with you, and though you may feel alone when you're going through a hard time, put your hope in God, for He has promised to be with you and to guide you.

When we are dealing with difficulties in life, and we all do at times, the devil wants us to be hopeless, not hopeful. He will try to get you to focus on your problem instead of on Jesus and His many promises. While Joshua was making his journey through the wilderness, God told him to keep his eyes on the promises and not to turn from them to the right or the left, that he might prosper in all of his ways (see Joshua 1:4–7). When trouble comes, don't let the cares and anxieties of the world make you hopeless. Be a prisoner of hope and receive a double reward from God.

> *Return to the stronghold [of security and prosperity], you prisoners of hope; even today do I declare that I will restore double your former prosperity to you.*
>
> Zechariah 9:12

I recently read about a man who was learning to fly airplanes. During one particular lesson, his instructor told him to put the plane into a steep and extended dive. The student did as he was instructed, but he wasn't prepared for what happened next. Shortly after he started the dive, the engine stalled and the plane began to plummet out of control. With panic in his eyes, the student looked at his instructor for help, but the instructor didn't say a word. The student quickly calmed himself, regained his composure, and corrected the situation according to his previous training—training that was being put to the test for the first time.

After the plane was level and they were safely flying again, the student turned to his instructor and began to vent his fears and frustrations. It seemed as if the instructor had disappeared while on the job, and his student wasn't happy about it. After listening to the outrage from his student, the flight instructor calmly replied, "There is no position you can get this airplane into that I cannot get you out of. If you want to learn to fly, go up there and do it again." Though the student had gone through a trying ordeal, and even though he felt alone for a few terrifying moments, his instructor had been there the whole time. He wasn't going to let anything happen to his student. He was actually using the adversity to teach and equip his student with skills he would need in the future.[1]

I share that story with you because there may be times in your life when you feel as if you are in a deep and extended dive, times when it feels like your engine has stalled and you are plummeting out of control. A marriage crumbles, a dream dies, a diagnosis is given, a child strays, a trust is broken, a job is lost. In difficult times like these, it's natural to feel a sense of panic and to wonder if you are all alone. But just because you may temporarily feel alone, afraid, and abandoned, that doesn't mean you are. God is right there with you; He has not left your side.

Deuteronomy 31:8 (NIV) says that God "will never leave you nor forsake you," and in Matthew 28:20 (NIV), Jesus promised, "I am with you always." These are just two of the many times in the Word of God where the Lord assures you He will never leave you to go through things alone. Even on your worst days, even in the midst of the most trying circumstances, know that you are not alone.

Get Your Hopes Up!

What are you most passionate about? What is the thing that makes you excited just thinking about it? Starting a nonprofit? Volunteering in your community? Building a company? Raising a family? Getting your degree? Many times the desires of your heart are so strong because God is the one who put them there. Whatever it is you are hoping for, submit that thing to God, ask for His direction, and if you feel a peace about it, take steps to make it happen. Following God is not about sitting back and waiting for it—

> *Following God is not about sitting back and waiting for it—it's about being courageous and going for it.*

it's about being courageous and going for it. Go ahead and get your hopes up...God is leading you to something better than you can imagine.

CHAPTER 3

Identify and Eliminate Every "Can't"

Praised (honored, blessed) be the God and Father of our Lord Jesus Christ (the Messiah)! By His boundless mercy we have been born again to an ever-living hope through the resurrection of Jesus Christ from the dead...

1 Peter 1:3

"A little more persistence, a little more effort, and what seemed a hopeless failure may turn to glorious success."

—Elbert Hubbard

In 1981, a self-made millionaire by the name of Eugene Lang returned to the inner-city elementary school he attended 50 years earlier. He was there to give a speech to the class of graduating sixth graders, but something the principal told him just before he took the stage disturbed Lang. The principal informed the successful businessman that, statistically, three-quarters of the school's students would never complete high school—they would drop out long before receiving a diploma. Lang planned to speak to the young students about the value of hard work and how it would lead to success, but when the principal told him that startling statistic, he quickly changed the content of his speech. Eugene Lang decided to do something radical.

As he stood before the sixth graders in this Harlem elementary school, Lang told the class how he witnessed Dr. Martin Luther King Jr.'s famous "I Have a Dream" speech at the March on Washington in 1963. He encouraged each student to dream their own dreams, and then he told the class he wanted to do something to help them see those dreams come true. That day, Lang made a deal with those young students: He promised to pay the college tuition of every sixth grader who stayed in school and received a high school diploma.

The lives of those young people changed that day. They had hope—many of them for the very first time. When interviewed later, one student said, "I had something to look forward to, something waiting for me. It was a golden feeling." Eugene Lang's promise turned into a school program, and his school program turned into a national movement. The *New York Times* ran a front-page story and *60 Minutes* aired a segment on the millionaire who brought hope to a group of inner-city children. Thousands of calls and letters began pouring in, and in 1986, Lang started the national I Have A Dream Foundation to help build I Have A Dream programs in schools around the country. Since then, over 200 programs have operated in 29 states, and over 15,000 students (called "Dreamers") have been helped.

And as for the 61 sixth graders—the original Dreamers—that Lang gave his impromptu speech to that early summer day in 1981? More than 90% went on to earn their high school diplomas, and most of those went on to pursue higher education. It was all due to the generosity of one businessman who just wanted to help a group of kids go higher.[1]

Hope is a powerful thing, but it doesn't thrive in an atmosphere of *can't*.

Before Lang made his promise to that group of poverty-stricken, inner-city children, many of them lived under a cloud of "can't." *We can't go to college*

> Hope is a powerful thing, but it doesn't thrive in an atmosphere of can't.

because we can't *afford the tuition costs. So why finish high school if college isn't even an option?* What Eugene Lang did was eliminate the *can't*. He didn't go to class for them, he didn't do their homework, he didn't build their projects, he didn't take their tests—they still had to do the necessary work. But he identified and eliminated the biggest *can't* they were facing—and that's when hope soared.

God's Response When You Think *I Can't*

As you began reading this book, you probably noticed I titled this first section "Hope to Go Higher." That's because I am convinced God wants to do bigger and better things in your life—He wants to take you higher. God wants you to experience a higher level of joy, a higher level of peace, a higher level of contentment, a higher level of hope, and the list goes on and on. Colossians 3:1–2 says:

> *If then you have been raised with Christ [to a new life, thus sharing His resurrection from the dead], aim at and seek the [rich, eternal treasures] that are above, where Christ is, seated at the right hand of God. And* **set your minds and keep them set on what is above (the higher things),** *not on the things that are on the earth (emphasis added).*

> With God, things don't get worse and worse, they get better and better—you don't sink lower and lower, you rise higher and higher.

With God, things don't get worse and worse, they get better and better—you don't sink lower and lower, you rise higher and higher.

That's why Proverbs 4:18 says the path of the righteous "is like the light of dawn, that shines more and more (brighter and clearer)" and why Isaiah 40:31 (NKJV) says those who wait for the Lord "shall mount up with wings like eagles." Your life in Christ can be a life that gets brighter each day, where you soar higher than you ever have before.

But one of the strongest and most effective obstacles that keeps you from experiencing the life God wants you to live is the mind-set of *can't*. *Can't* is an unforgiving cage designed to keep you from rising to your full potential. Picture the majestic bald eagle—a bird meant to glide on the wings of the wind—perched in a cramped cage, watching other eagles soar. This is what happens when you live with a mind-set of *can't*. Instead of living the life you were designed to live, you are stuck in an enclosure of restrictions and limitations. I can't *control my temper*. I can't *find a job*. I can't *get past that hurt*. I can't *keep going*. I can't *get along with my spouse*. I can't *make myself vulnerable again*. I can't *figure this out*. I can't *raise these children alone*. I can't *believe this is happening*. I can't…I can't… I can't. We could go on and on. There is seemingly no end to the things people think they can't do.

But did you notice an important factor in the previous list of thoughts? I. I can't…I can't…I can't. I…I…I. *Can't* is a mind-set that focuses on self. It doesn't consider help from others, and it certainly doesn't consider help from God. *Can't* looks at the weakest parts of us and draws this hopeless conclusion: I can't do it.

This is nothing new. The men and women in the Bible dealt with this same attitude. Sarah thought, *I can't bear children; I'm too old* (see Genesis 18:10–12). Moses thought, *I can't stand before Pharaoh; I don't speak well* (see Exodus 6:30). Gideon thought, *I can't lead Israel; I'm the least in my family* (see Judges 6:15). Esther thought, *I can't save my people; I will never get an audience with the king* (see Esther 4:11). Isaiah thought, *I can't prophesy; I am a man of unclean lips* (see Isaiah 6:5–7). The disciples thought, *We can't feed this crowd; all we have are five loaves of bread and two fish* (see Matthew 14:15–18). In each of these circumstances, *can't* stood as a self-built cage, trying to keep these men and women from fulfilling God's plan for their lives.

But God never intended for Sarah, Moses, Gideon, Esther, Isaiah, or the disciples to do anything in their own strength, according to their own ability. He knew they couldn't...but that didn't matter, because He *could*. Through Christ we can do anything we need to do. We can face anything!

> *I have strength for all things in Christ Who empowers me [I am ready for anything and equal to anything through Him Who infuses inner strength into me; I am self-sufficient in Christ's sufficiency].*
>
> Philippians 4:13

It was true: Sarah was too old to have children; Moses couldn't convince Pharaoh on his own; Gideon was unqualified to lead an army; Esther hadn't been summoned before the king; Isaiah was a man of unclean lips; and the disciples didn't have enough food to feed the crowd. But God intended to overcome every *can't* in order to fulfill His plan and purpose. All these men and women had to do was to identify and eliminate their "I can't" mind-sets. Instead of focusing on their weaknesses, they chose to focus on God's strength, and the results were miraculous. God did amazing things in their lives and through their faith and obedience.

The same is true for you. I recognize there are things you are facing today that may have you thinking *I just can't do it. I can't deal with this situation any longer. I can't take this another day. I can't wait for an answer. I can't find a way to forgive. If you knew what I was going through, you would understand. I just can't do it.* But I want to tell you that God knows you can't...and that doesn't matter, because He *can*.

> *Jesus glanced around at them and said, With men [it is] impossible, but not with God; for all things are possible with God.*
>
> Mark 10:27

Have a "Can Do" Attitude

Maybe you've gone through life thinking *I can't* because that's what others have told you. Maybe you heard "you can't" so many times you began to internalize it and personalize it, and somewhere along the way "you can't" turned into *I can't.* It's sad to think there are many people who enjoy telling others what they cannot do. And sometimes these people are the people who are closest to you. A teacher, a sibling, a church leader, a parent, a friend, a person you respect greatly—it can be disheartening when these people overlook your potential. It can disillusion and debilitate us if we allow it to, but we can also choose an alternate course. We can choose to believe God when He says that we can!

If no one else has told you previously, hear God saying now "You can!" Those are powerful words for you to hear and believe, because as I like to say, "Miracles come in cans." You *can* overcome. You *can* make it through. You *can* forgive. You *can* raise godly children. You *can* have a happy marriage. You *can* experience joy. You *can* meet your goal. You *can* be disciplined. You *can* move on. You *can*...you *can*...you *can.*

When facing any challenge—no matter how big it may seem—God will give you all the strength you need. Armed with God's power, you can identify and eliminate every *can't* in your life and replace it with a *can.* " 'Can do' is the parent of 'Have done.' " (Israelmore Ayivor)

> *When facing any challenge—no matter how big it may seem—God will give you all the strength you need.*

In his book titled *The Anatomy of an Illness: As Perceived by the Patient*, Norman Cousins tells the story of being hospitalized with a rare and debilitating disease. The doctors told him it was incurable—he would be sick and in pain the rest of his life. Cousins checked himself out of the hospital and did something unusual.

Knowing that negative thoughts and emotions have damaging effects on the body, Cousins decided to eliminate the negative and amplify the positive in his situation. He decided he needed large doses of hope, love, joy, and laughter. Cousins started spending time each day watching old Marx Brothers films and watching classic reruns of *Candid Camera*. It sounds simple enough, but Cousins decided he would rather laugh in the midst of his condition than cry from the pain of it. What he discovered was that 10 minutes of laughter would give him two hours of pain-free sleep. Amazingly, over time, his disease was reversed, and the story of his recovery appeared in the *New England Journal of Medicine*. Thousands of doctors wrote Cousins, thanking him for sharing his experiment, and Hollywood even made a movie about it.[2]

I thank God for doctors and the advancements in medical technology we have today. I don't tell you Norman Cousins' story to discourage you from going to the doctor. I share that story as a practical example of how powerful it is when you eliminate the negative attitudes and mind-sets that try to hold you down. In the case of Norman Cousins, it even affected his physical health. Just think of how your life can change when you shed the negativity of "I can't" and embrace the hope of "I can." When you choose to focus on the things you can do in Christ instead of the things you can't do on your own, it will change your thoughts, your words, your outlook, and your attitude—it will change your life. Those who hope in God will never be disappointed or put to shame (see Romans 5:4–5).

> Just think of how your life can change when you shed the negativity of "I can't" and embrace the hope of "I can."

Doing the Impossible

With God's help, we can do what seems impossible if we will not be afraid to try.

Some of the world's most well-known people had a "can do" attitude and they did amazing things. Here are quotes from a few of them:

It's kind of fun to do the impossible.
Walt Disney

There is nothing impossible to him who will try.
Alexander the Great

Every noble work is at first impossible.
Thomas Carlyle

The only place that your dream becomes impossible is in your own thinking.
Robert H. Schuller

We would accomplish many more things if we did not think of them as impossible.
Vince Lombardi

The word impossible is not in my dictionary.
Napoleon Bonaparte

It always seems impossible until it is done.
Nelson Mandela

Don't allow your mind to become a hindrance to the things you can accomplish in life. Think big, as God does! You are going to think something, so why think something little? I believe a lot of people are afraid to think big because they don't want to be disappointed, but I would rather take a chance on being disappointed occasionally than live a disappointing life because I never tried.

Everything that has never been done is impossible until someone does it, so why can't it be you?

We have a successful prison ministry, and over the past 16 years, our team that visits prisons has been in over 3,200 prisons and distributed 2.7 million of my books along with hygiene gift bags. We have visited every state prison in the United States, and yet when we first attempted it, we were told it was impossible. The first state prison board we contacted for permission to go into every prison in that state said, "That is impossible—nobody has ever done that!"

Dare to dream and your dreams just might come true! Dream of nothing and you are sure to get everything you failed to dream. You can read this book and hopefully finish it with the thought *That was a good book. I feel more hopeful.* But I urge you not to merely continue on with life as usual. Let the words in this book be a catalyst for greater things in your life. Have bigger hopes, dream big, and think big. Somebody is going to do it, and it may as well be you!

Get Your Hopes Up!

I believe God wants to help you break free from the cage of *can't*. You can receive hope today, maybe for the first time. Whatever challenge or opportunity lies before you, you can succeed—because God is with you, and He will give you all the strength you need. The negative words from others are no match for the promises of God and His presence in your life. When God is for you, it doesn't matter who or what is against you (see Romans 8:31).

Go ahead and get your hopes up. You may have failed in the past, but you can overcome today. You may have made mistakes in the past, but you can make wise decisions today. You may have given up in the past, but you can persevere today. You may have been hesitant in the past, but you can be bold today. People may have told you "you can't" in the past, but today, you can. Break out of the cage that has kept you from enjoying God's best in your life. Soar higher into the plans and purposes He has for you. And if things get difficult, don't worry or be afraid. You CAN do it!

CHAPTER 4

The Energy of Hope

*We remember before our God and Father your work
produced by faith, your labor prompted by love,
and your endurance inspired by hope in our Lord
Jesus Christ.*

1 Thessalonians 1:3 NIV

"Hope is sweet-minded and sweet-eyed. It draws pictures;
it weaves fancies; it fills the future with delight."
—Henry Ward Beecher

When I talk to people about hope, I've discovered many of them
have a misconception as to what hope really is. And if you don't
understand what something is or how it works, things can fall apart
quickly.

This reminds me of a funny story someone shared with me about
the challenges of coaching his four-year-old son's soccer team. He
said he showed up at the soccer fields for the first practice of the
season a little nervous. He'd never coached soccer before, and none
of the children had ever played soccer before, so he knew he had his
work cut out for him. The kids all showed up on time, wearing their
brand-new cleats, kicking their shiny, multicolored soccer balls.
Everyone seemed excited.

This rookie coach gathered the four-year-old teammates into
a huddle while proud and doting parents snapped picture after

picture on their phones, quickly posting "First practice of the year!" photos to social media sites for all to see. The coach explained to the children they were going to have a "great season," and in every practice they were going to play "fun games" to help each of them learn the skills of soccer. The kids cheered at the mention of games, so the coach decided to begin practice with a relay drill. He said, "Okay, kids. Today we're going to have a relay race!" The kids shouted in unison, "Hooray!" Feeling confident by the enthusiastic response of these preschoolers, the coach lined the children up in two lines, instructing them to dribble the ball down to the cone and then dribble back. He said, "It's just like a relay race, the only difference is you're kicking a soccer ball." Again the kids squealed in delight.

"Are you ready, kids?" the coach exclaimed. "Yeeeesssss!" the kids shouted in unison. "On your mark...Get set...GO!"

When the coach yelled, "GO!" pandemonium broke loose. Instead of the first player from each line running down to the cone while the other children waited their turns (normal relay race behavior), all of the children began sprinting in every direction at once. They heard "GO"...so they went! There was no order, no structure—just chaos. It took the coach, with the help of several bewildered but laughing parents, a solid 10 minutes to corral the children—pulling some off the goal posts, retrieving others from the concession stand, and finding one confused child on another field trying to join a rival team.

When the coach got home from practice that night, feeling more tired than he'd ever felt in his life, he told his wife (an elementary school teacher) about the fiasco. "I lined them up," he said, "I explained we were going to have a relay race. I shouted, 'On your mark...get set...GO!' How could that go wrong?" His wife laughed to herself and explained to her confused husband that the children on his team were only four years old; they weren't in elementary school yet. These children probably hadn't been taught the rules of a relay race because they hadn't been in group settings with team competitions. The only things those preschoolers heard were "race" and "GO!"—so that's exactly what they did. They misunderstood the race, and the result was frustration and disorder.

As I think about that story, I realize that just as those children misunderstood the race, many people misunderstand hope, and the result is frustration and disorder. There are a lot of people who think hope is a passive word—something of a lazy emotion. They incorrectly assume if they sit around passively, just hoping things will get better, then maybe they will. But hope is not a sit-back-and-do-nothing feeling. It's more than a daydream or a wishful thought. If this is your understanding of hope, you're going to be uncertain about what you want and are not likely to get it.

Hope energizes us and motivates us to take action. As I said before, it's the happy, confident expectation of good, and that happy, confident expectation of good causes you to step out in faith and to act in obedience with God's Word. Hope is too exciting to be passive. Hope believes boldly, decides daringly, speaks firmly, and perseveres passionately.

> Hope is too exciting to be passive.

There is no inaction with hope, because there is no inaction with God. God is always moving and working in your life, and He wants you to move in obedience with Him. A lazy, procrastinating, passive person is never a happy person. When you understand the power of hope, you're a person ready and excited to move in faith and do what needs to be done when the time is right.

At times we may be waiting on God, but true waiting is not passive, it is very active in the spirit realm. We are *expecting* God to do great things. There are countless Scripture verses that speak of waiting on God, and in the Amplified translation of the Bible, each of those places says to "wait on and expect the Lord." I love that because it clarifies that we need to be actively expecting God to work in our lives. We need to be ready to move at a moment's notice from God, and while we are waiting, we are full of hopeful confidence that God is planning something big and wonderful for us. All you need to do is think of a pregnant woman who is expecting a baby! She is planning, dreaming, preparing, talking about, and thinking continually about the baby who is on the way.

Run to the Battle, Not Away from It!

When you read the book of Psalms, one of the first things you notice is that David was a man full of hope and expectation. You can hear it in the lyrics he wrote. Here are just a few examples:

> *Be strong and let your heart take courage, all you who wait for and* **hope for and expect the Lord***!*
>
> Psalm 31:24 (emphasis added)

> *Yes, let none who trust and* **wait hopefully and look for You** *be put to shame or be disappointed…*
>
> Psalm 25:3 (emphasis added)

> *And now, Lord, what do I wait for and expect?* **My hope and expectation are in You***.*
>
> Psalm 39:7 (emphasis added)

Whether he was tending sheep in the fields, leading a band of renegade soldiers, or ruling as king over Israel, David always lived with hope that God was going to do something amazing in his life. But David's hope didn't allow him to sit back and do nothing. In fact, the opposite is true. His hope stirred him to action. David trusted that God was going to do something miraculous, but he knew he was in partnership with God and that he needed to be obediently active. That's why we often see David asking for God's direction and then boldly taking steps of faith (see 1 Chronicles 14:10, 1 Chronicles 14:14, 1 Samuel 23:2, 2 Samuel 2:1).

Can you imagine if David had been passive, lacking enthusiasm, and undisciplined when he faced Goliath? Imagine David saying to himself *Well, I sure hope God does something. I'm just going to sit here in the trenches with the rest of the guys. Let's hope God sends lightning to strike this giant.* If that had been his attitude, God would have used someone else to defeat Goliath. God was looking for someone who would be willing to do his part—someone whose hope would stir him to action. David was that person!

When David showed up on the front lines to bring supplies to his brothers, and he heard the Philistine giant cursing God and taunting the armies of Israel, instantly, he got his hopes up. He said to the men around him, "What shall be done for the man who kills this Philistine and takes away the reproach from Israel?" (1 Samuel 17:26). He wasn't thinking about defeat; he wasn't thinking about failure; he wasn't thinking about the odds stacked against him—he was hopeful that he could succeed and the battle could be won.

That hope moved David to action. Between the time he first felt hope and the time the victory was actually won, look at the action steps he took: David resisted the criticism from his brother who tried to belittle and discourage him (vv. 28–30); he persuaded King Saul to let him fight (vv. 32–37); he tried on Saul's armor but decided not to use it (vv. 38–39); he chose five stones as ammunition for his slingshot (v. 40); he defied Goliath, predicting victory (vv. 45–47); and he ran to the battle (v. 48). David didn't have an attitude that said *Well, I sure hope things work out. Let's just wait and see.* He had an attitude that said *My hope is in God. Let's go win this battle!* David didn't run away from the battle or hide from it like the soldiers were doing; he ran toward it full of hope and faith that through God he could win against the giant. David had a positive expectation that something good was going to happen!

The Opportunity of Hope

You can have the same kind of attitude David had. You can use the hope that is building in your heart as you read this book to cause you to seek God's direction, step out in faith, and boldly do what God has put in your heart to do. God wants to do wonderful things in your life, but He won't do them if you are hopeless and negative—God wants you to take part in the miracle by being energetic and full of positive expectation. You might think *I wish I felt hopeful, Joyce, but I just don't.* Hope isn't something we wait to feel, it is something we decide to have.

> Hope isn't something we wait to feel, it is something we decide to have.

Be hopeful on purpose! Hope is a powerful, supernatural opportunity that you don't want to miss! A great deal of our energy is connected to our thinking, so if we think hopeful thoughts, our energy will increase, just as it would decrease if we thought hopeless things.

Some people *hope* God will do something to change their situation, yet they never take any action themselves. For example, people won't find a job if they don't go look for one. There are also people who take action, but they are hopeless and negative about the outcome. Neither of these types of people will obtain what they want, but there are those rare individuals who have a God-inspired dream; they pray and take action as God leads, and they remain hopeful no matter how long it takes for them to see their dreams fulfilled.

All through the Bible, we see God's people seizing supernatural opportunities and participating in their miracles. When God promised to bring down the walls of Jericho, the Israelites marched around the city, shouted in triumph, and fought the battle...action steps! As Jesus prepared to feed the 5,000, the disciples organized the crowd and passed out the food...action steps! Before Jesus healed the woman with the issue of blood, she pressed through the crowd and touched the hem of His garment…action steps! When the Holy Spirit fell on the Day of Pentecost, Peter stood before the people and preached the Gospel…action steps! If the men and women of the Bible can seize their opportunities and take decisive action steps, you and I can do the same thing.

In your life, it may look like this…

If you are hopeful for a new career, working in a field that would be an exciting, new challenge for you, let that hope stir you to action. Maybe you can take classes to broaden your knowledge in ways that could benefit you in this new profession. Perhaps you can talk to people who are currently on that career path, asking them what you can do to prepare yourself. Then, when you are properly prepared, aggressively look for a job and do it with hope in your heart and positive words coming out of your mouth.

If you are lacking energy and are often sick and you are hopeful for improved health, let that hope stir you to action. Maybe you could join a local gym and begin a new exercise routine. Perhaps there are some dietary habits or sleeping patterns you could change that would increase your energy levels. Perhaps it would be as simple as limiting your caffeine intake. It is easy to sit back and wait for God to do something, but don't fail to ask God if there is any action He wants you to take.

If you are hoping that a struggling relationship will improve, let that hope stir you to action. Instead of waiting for the other person to take a step, you take a step. Maybe you can write that person a thoughtful note or an encouraging email. Perhaps you can take that person out for coffee and apologize for something you may have done to cause an offense.

If you are hopeful that your finances will improve, hopeful that you can get past living paycheck to paycheck, let that hope stir you to action. Maybe you can put together a budget—or reevaluate your current budget—to monitor where your money is going. Perhaps you can meet with your boss and ask for new opportunities at work that will increase your salary along with the company's profits.

First be clear about what it is that you want or need. Pray about it in faith, and be full of hope as you wait on God. Be sure to walk in prompt obedience to any direction the Holy Spirit gives you. Some people pray and then doubt that what they ask for will ever happen. Those prayers are not answered. God said to "pray and do not doubt" (see James 1:6). The way to keep doubt from getting into your heart and mind is to stay filled with hope and positive expectation. Hope should not be a one-time thing, or a "here and there" thing. Hope should be a constant in our lives!

Prayerfully consider what steps God would have you take in order to see your dreams fulfilled. If it is something that is from the Lord, He will guide you and bless your hard work. God put a dream in my heart about teaching His Word and helping other people, and I can honestly say that I have not been inactive since that time. I have had many discouraging days and difficult times, but over the years I have learned to remain filled with hope. It has always made my life better and made me a better person. As you take action toward the fulfillment of your dreams and goals, you can pray the same thing Moses prayed: *And let the beauty and delightfulness and favor of the Lord our God be upon us; confirm and establish the work of our hands—yes, the work of our hands, confirm and establish it* (Psalm 90:17). Moses didn't ask God to bless his inactive passivity; he asked that his work would be blessed.

God Uses Broken Vessels

Maybe you're reading this chapter and you're painfully aware of the times you've messed up while taking a step in the past. Maybe there were opportunities when you set out with great intentions, excited to take bold steps and really make things happen, but they didn't work out. If that's how you're feeling, I can certainly understand where you're coming from. There have been many days when I tried

> We shouldn't let the failures in our past keep us from trying again in the future.

my best, but instead of making things better, I felt like I actually made things worse. I think we all have experienced days like that. But we shouldn't let the failures in our past keep us from trying again in the future.

God knows we have limitations and shortcomings. Our failures don't surprise Him, and they don't keep Him from working in our lives. As a matter of fact, God will often use our limitations to showcase His power. I came across a story that illustrates what I mean:

A water-bearer in India had two large pots hanging at the ends of a pole that he carried across his neck. One of the pots was perfect and always delivered a full portion of water at the end of the long walk from the stream to the master's house. The other pot had a crack in it, and by the time it reached its destination, it was only half full. Every day for two years the water-bearer delivered only one and one-half pots of water to the master's house. Of course, the perfect pot was proud of its accomplishments—perfect to the end for which it was made. The poor little cracked pot was ashamed of its imperfections and miserable that it could accomplish only half of what it had been designed to do. After two years of what the imperfect pot perceived to be a bitter failure, it spoke to the water-bearer and said, "I am ashamed of myself and I want to apologize to you."

"Why?" asked the water-bearer. "What are you ashamed of?"

"Well, for these past two years, I have been able to deliver only half a load of water each day because this crack in my side allows water to leak out the whole way back to the master's house. Because of my flaws, you have to do all this work without getting the full value of your efforts," the pot said.

The water-bearer felt sorry for the old cracked pot, and in his compassion he said, "As we return to the master's house, I want you to notice the beautiful flowers along the path." Indeed, as they went up the hill, the old cracked pot noticed the beautiful wildflowers on the side of the path. But at the end of the trail, it still felt bad because half of its load had leaked out once again.

Then the water-bearer said to the pot, "Did you notice that there were flowers only on your side of the path and not on the other pot's side? That's because I've always known about your flaw and took advantage of it by planting flower seeds on your side of the path. Every day as we walked back from the stream, you watered those seeds, and for two years I have picked these beautiful flowers to decorate my master's table. Without you being just what you are, he would not have had this beauty to grace his house."[1]

Like that cracked pot, you too can accomplish wonderful things. It doesn't matter that you have flaws and limitations. Don't let what you perceive to be a weakness keep you from taking bold steps inspired by hope. 2 Corinthians 12:10 says: "...When I am weak [in human strength], then am I [truly] strong (able, powerful in divine strength).'' Isn't that comforting to know? Even when you're weak, you're strong because God is with you. He is using every part of your life—even the cracks—to create something beautiful.

Get Your Hopes Up!

Hope is exciting because you have a part to play. You don't have to sit back, just waiting for an answer to fall from the sky. You can take your hopes to God, ask Him for His wisdom, guidance, and direction, and then take real and practical steps toward your goal. It doesn't matter how difficult the task may seem or what odds are stacked against you; let hope stir you to action, one day at a time. In addition to obediently doing what you feel God is leading you to do, you can aggressively thank God that He is working in your life. You can always maintain a positive attitude and speak positive words out of your mouth. You can recall other victories you have had in your life in the past and be encouraged by them. Victory will require determination and discipline, but the results will be dynamic. So go ahead and get your hopes up. God helped David defeat a giant. He can do the same for you.

CHAPTER 5

Getting to Know the New You

And we all, who with unveiled faces contemplate the Lord's glory, are being transformed into his image with ever-increasing glory, which comes from the Lord, who is the Spirit.

2 Corinthians 3:18 (NIV)

"There are three things extremely hard: steel, a diamond, and to know one's self."

—Benjamin Franklin

Change isn't easy—even good change takes some getting used to. When God changes us, it takes time for us to become confident that we really have changed. The apostle Paul knew that was true.

When we think of Paul, we think of a spiritual giant, author of much of the New Testament. When someone stands up in church and says, "Let's read what Paul said in Romans," or "As Paul said in the book of Galatians…" no one questions it. But there was a time when Paul was a guy everyone questioned. He wasn't the great apostle; he was just a man with a new name and a bad reputation: *Pharisee of Pharisees. Persecutor of the early church. Someone who can't be trusted.* So I wonder if there was an adjustment period—a time when Paul felt more like Saul than Paul. I wonder if it took time for Paul to let go of Saul. I wonder if he ever shook someone's hand and said, "Hi. I'm Saul…er…um…I mean, Paul. I'm Paul."

Most women who have been married know a name change can require some getting used to. You were Mary Smith, but now you're Mary Styborski. You used to be Sally Jones, but now you're Sally Rigglestein. It takes time to get comfortable with a new name, but keep in mind, Paul was dealing with more than just a name change—Paul was embracing a change of heart and nature as well. Imagine him saying *"Hi. I'm Paul. I'm a follower of Jesus now. I'd like to tell you about Him."* People must have looked at this Christian-persecuting-Pharisee-turned-preacher and thought *Wait a second. This is that Saul guy. I've heard about him. He persecutes and arrests Christians… I don't trust him and I find it hard to believe he has really changed!*

While we can only speculate how random people on the streets reacted to Paul's new identity, the Bible tells us exactly how the disciples reacted—they didn't buy it. They weren't convinced Paul was a new man. Acts 9:26 says: "And when [Paul] had arrived in Jerusalem, he tried to associate himself with the disciples; but they were all afraid of him, for they did not believe he really was a disciple." It's only because Barnabas stood before the disciples and vouched for Paul's character that they even considered accepting him. Of course, we know they eventually did, and the rest of the story is biblical history. But there is one phrase in the previous verse that I want to call to your attention: "They did not believe he really was a disciple." The only thing that could make that phrase more tragic is if it said: Paul *did not believe he really was a disciple.*

You see, Paul couldn't control what the disciples thought. Barnabas had to talk to the disciples, and God had to change their hearts. That was all out of Paul's hands. The only thing Paul could control was his own attitude. Truth be told, it probably didn't matter what everybody else believed. What really mattered was what *Paul* believed. If he never embraced the new person he was in Christ, he would never have lived out his destiny. Can you imagine Paul walking around thinking *I wish I could travel and preach the Word of God.*

That's what is in my heart to do. But I was a persecutor of the church. I'll always be Saul. Or if he thought *I got a late start in life. There's no way I can do all the things I wish I could do for God. I was Saul for way too long.* If that had been his attitude, Paul would have been miserable, and he would not have accomplished all God had for him to do.

But once God began working in his life, Paul understood that he was no longer Saul, so he stopped living like Saul. He no longer thought like a Pharisee, talked like a Pharisee, or acted like a Pharisee. Things were different now. He had been changed. He had been given hope. And he chose to act like it.

It was Paul who, under the inspiration of the Holy Spirit, wrote:

Therefore if any person is [ingrafted] in Christ (the Messiah) he is a new creation (a new creature altogether); the old [previous moral and spiritual condition] has passed away. **Behold, the fresh and new has come!**

2 Corinthians 5:17 (emphasis added)

For neither is circumcision [now] of any importance, nor uncircumcision, **but [only] a new creation [the result of a new birth and a new nature in Christ Jesus, the Messiah].**

Galatians 6:15 (emphasis added)

Paul was full of hope, and he was excited about his life because "the fresh and new" had come—he now had a "new nature in Christ Jesus." Paul no longer walked around thinking, speaking, worrying, working, and acting like Saul. He had been changed. Paul embraced the new things God was doing in his life, the new opportunities that were before him, and the new person God had destined him to be.

Let Go of the Old You

What was true in Paul's life is true in your life as well. You too are a "new creation [the result of a new birth and a new nature in Christ Jesus]," and you too can experience that "the fresh and new has come." You're not the person you used to be. God has done so much in your life—He has changed you. I am sure that, like me, you are a long way from perfect, but I am also sure that you have made progress and that you have come a long way toward positive change. If you were to stop and think about who you used to be—the things you used to struggle with—you'd get pretty excited about how far God has brought you.

> If you were to stop and think about who you used to be—the things you used to struggle with—you'd get pretty excited about how far God has brought you.

My husband, Dave, was talking to me just this morning about a man he plays golf with. This man shared with Dave that his wife, although a Christian, has never gotten over her abusive childhood. Over the years she has had mental and emotional problems and is now having lots of physical problems due to the internal stress she lives under. As Dave and I talked about it and discussed why some people with the exact same past get completely well, while others do not, we both came to the same conclusion. In order to recover from the pain of the past, we must truly believe that we are new creatures in Christ. We must completely let go of the old people that we were and learn to live the resurrection life that Jesus has provided. We must stop identifying with the sinful, wounded, or abused person that we used to be and start identifying with the new person God has made us in Christ.

In the life of the believer, hope is rooted in the understanding that God changes things. Change, rebirth, transformation: This is the good news of the Gospel. On your own, you were lost, broken, far from God, and without hope. But because of His great love, God sent Jesus so you could be found, healed, reconciled to Him, and your hope could be restored. Salvation is about change—change made possible because of God's love for you and for me.

Not only is salvation about change, but your daily walk with God is too. All through Scripture, whenever individuals had an encounter with God, change occurred. Abram became Abraham (see Genesis 17:5). Sarai became Sarah (see Genesis 17:15). Jacob became Israel (see Genesis 32:28). Simon became Peter (see John 1:42). Saul became Paul (see Acts 13:9). And it's not just names that changed—the direction of people's lives changed. A shepherd became a king. A fugitive became a nation's leader. Fishermen became disciples. A Pharisee became an apostle.

But it's important to notice that, along with Paul, when God brought about change in the lives of these men and women, they embraced the new people God created them to be. David didn't walk around with a shepherd boy's mentality; he embraced his role as king. Moses no longer hid in fear from Pharaoh; he boldly declared, "Let my people go!" Peter was no longer afraid; he stood up and preached to thousands on the Day of Pentecost. Each person embraced what God had done—and what He was doing—in their lives…and so can you. As a matter of fact, if you don't embrace it, you will always struggle and live on a low level of life, far from the exciting, powerful life that is yours in Jesus.

Let me ask you: Do you believe God loves you unconditionally? Do you believe ALL your sins are forgiven? Do you believe you are a new creature with a new heart and spirit? Have you accepted yourself? Do you like yourself? Do you believe the future holds exciting things for you?

If you do believe these things, then let me congratulate you because you are well on your way to amazingly good things. If you don't believe these things, then it is time to study God's Word until you do. Believe the promises in God's Word more than you believe how you feel, and don't ever give up until you have victory. Renew

your mind to new creation realities. Things like you are the righteousness of God in Christ! You are justified and sanctified through

> When you realize you
> are a new person, you
> have a new hope.

the blood of Jesus! You have God-given
talents and abilities! God lives in you
and He will never leave you or forsake
you! When you realize you are a new
person, you have a new hope.

The person you used to be, the mistakes you used to make, the
unjust things that have happened to you, the struggles you used to
go through—those things don't have to hold you back any longer.
Don't walk around telling yourself *I have an anger problem. I just
can't control my temper.* No, that was the old you. God has changed
you inside, and you are being transformed by His power within
you. You are now a person full of the peace and joy of the Lord.
Embrace that person. We start by believing the good news of the
Gospel, and then we renew our minds by studying God's Word, and
we start living in the reality of the new person we are in Christ.

Instead of going through life with a victim mentality, telling yourself *Well, I just can't trust anyone. I can never have a healthy relationship because of the dysfunction of my past,* or *I am no good,* embrace
the healing power of God in your life. You are a new person. He is
healing every wound and restoring what you lost. In fact, He is going
to give you double blessings for the things that were taken from you
(see Isaiah 61:7). If you were hurt in the past, that doesn't make you
a victim for the rest of your life. You can overcome that pain and
live an overcoming, victorious life. You
are a new creation in Christ, full of new
strength and new hope. Remember,
your history is not your destiny!

> You can confidently go
> through each day know-
> ing you're stronger than
> you used to be, because
> every day God is doing
> a great work in your life.

You can confidently go through each
day knowing you're stronger than you
used to be, because every day God is
doing a great work in your life. That

doesn't mean you've accomplished everything you want to accomplish, and it doesn't mean you do everything perfectly now, but it does mean you can have a new hope. A hope that inspires you to say, like Paul: "Not that I have now attained [this ideal], or have already been made perfect, but I press on to lay hold of (grasp) and make my own, that for which Christ Jesus (the Messiah) has laid hold of me and made me His own" (Philippians 3:12).

Don't spend another day saying "I can't do it," "I won't make it," or "I'm not good enough." Those are hopeless words. Maybe those things described the old you, but they certainly don't describe the new you in Christ. You are a child of God. You are more than a conqueror. You are the head and not the tail. You are the righteousness of God in Christ Jesus. Greater is He who is in you than he who is in the world.

The New You Has an Inheritance

When you became a believer, you came into a new family—the family of God. Now you have brothers and sisters in Christ who understand what you're going through and who can encourage you along the way, and you have a heavenly Father who will never leave you. One of the many blessings you receive from your heavenly Father is an inheritance. Ephesians 1:18 says:

> *By having the eyes of your heart flooded with light, so that you can know and understand the hope to which He has called you, and* **how rich is His glorious inheritance** *in the saints (His set-apart ones) . . . (emphasis added)*

Through Christ, an inheritance is provided for each of us. That means we're not hired servants working to earn something from God, but we are His children and we are inheritors. As joint heirs with Christ, we get what He earned and sacrificed for us. The Bible says

> *As joint heirs with Christ, we get what He earned and sacrificed for us. The Bible says that everything that is His is now ours (see John 16:15).*

that everything that is His is now ours (see John 16:15). And when you realize you have an inheritance from God, it changes the way you view things. Your problems don't seem as big, your frustrations don't seem as significant, the future doesn't seem so frightening—you can be joyful and full of hope, because God has already provided everything you need!

We serve a good God, and He wants to flood your life with good things. If you go through each day worrying about how a bill is going to be paid, afraid you're not going to get the promotion at work, bitter about what someone said behind your back, you're not living like a child who understands you have an inheritance. Worry, fear, and bitterness are character traits of the old you. The new you can trust, be confident, and forgive, because you believe God can take anything that happens to you and work it out for your good—He has good things stored up for you. If someone else gets that promotion, God obviously has something better for you. Don't worry or get depressed. Embrace the new you—realize you have a great inheritance in God—and get your hopes up about what God is going to teach you and how He is going to provide for you through this situation. If someone says something bad about you, instead of getting bitter, ask God how to handle the situation. In the past, you might have lost your cool and told that person off, but that was the old you. God has brought you a long way since then. You have an inheritance in Him, and He can turn that situation into something good.

Newer and Even Bigger Expectations

We began this book by talking about expectations. And as we end this chapter and this first section, I want to encourage you to actually begin raising those expectations. Have a hope to go higher!

The more hope you have, the easier it will be to walk by faith. I pray that God has been building your faith throughout these first five chapters—that's why I think it's time to expect even more from God. He loves you so much and wants to bless your life beyond measure (see Ephesians 3:20).

We say that a pregnant woman is "expecting." That's why she starts making plans. She is acting on her expectation—buying clothes, bottles, setting up the crib, and preparing the nursery. We need to act like people who are expecting. We should get up in the morning making plans for God to do something great. With God's help, we can think *Today may be the day. This is the day the Lord has made, and something great is bound to happen to me.* Even if God

> *We should get up in the morning making plans for God to do something great.*

doesn't do exactly the thing you're asking for, try to broaden your view. Maybe you're asking for something and God's got something better in mind. Don't just ask for good; believe and hope for great.

Wake up each day saying "I have a happy and confident expectation that something amazing is going to happen today. My spouse is going to bless me. My kids are going to behave. I'm going to get great news at work. God is going to give me an opportunity to bless someone. A blessing is going to come in the mail. I'm going to experience a breakthrough today." Don't be afraid to trust, believe, and speak blessings over your day from the moment you wake up. I have decided to refer to this book as "The Happy Book." I believe anyone who reads it will become happier than ever before. Hope is a joyful and confident expectation that something good is about to happen!

Hope removes the limits from our expectations. Are you expecting a little or a lot from the Lord? You may be halfway hoping God will do something. You may be halfway believing for something good, but I want to challenge you to completely and wholeheartedly believe for greater things than ever before. I want to challenge you to believe that God can use you in greater ways. If you write songs, why can't God give you the greatest song that's ever been written? If you preach the Word, why can't God give you a message so powerful, so awesome, that every time it's preached, it sets captives free? If you're raising children, why can't your children grow up to be world changers? Why can't you be promoted at your job? Why can't you meet the person you are to marry and have an amazingly great life? Why can't you overcome that hurt? Why can't you make a difference in the lives of those around you? It's time to start living with a new level of hopeful expectation. Believe that if anything good can happen to anyone, then it can happen to you!

> *If anything good can happen to anyone, then it can happen to you!*

Get Your Hopes Up!

When you look in the mirror today, I hope you'll see yourself as God sees you. You aren't a lost, broken, defeated, helpless person. You aren't a person unable to control your mind or emotions, and you aren't a person who can't get past your past. You are so much more than those things! You are more than a conqueror (see Romans 8:37). You are a new creation in Christ, and God is working in your life. Little by little, one day at a time, God is changing you. You can live differently than you used to because you're an overcomer. Believe these truths. Go ahead and get your hopes up!

SECTION II

HOPE WHEN YOU'RE HURTING

. . . .

[Now] we have this [hope] as a sure and steadfast anchor of the soul...

Hebrews 6:19

We need hope all the time, but especially when we are hurting. Hope seems more elusive when we are in the midst of difficulty or personal pain of any kind. However, it is vital not to use "I'm going through tough times" as an excuse to be discouraged, depressed, and hopeless.

Although it is more difficult, it is also more important than ever to be hopeful during times of struggle. God wants to bring us through, not see us get stuck in the pain.

When loss comes, let's deal with the loss and, in the process, not lose ourselves. When tragedy comes, let's grieve properly and not give way to the spirit of grief that will turn our entire life into a tragedy. When we are disappointed, let's get reappointed. When we are depressed, let's look up because we will all feel better if we hold our heads up high!

Everything about Jesus is up! He came from Heaven, He returned to Heaven when His work here was done, and we are promised that

He will come again in the clouds and every eye will see Him. He lifts our heads, our spirits, and our lives. On the other hand, we do have an enemy called Lucifer, Satan, the great deceiver, or the devil, and everything he offers is something down. He offers depression, discouragement, dejection, disease, despair, despondency, divorce, death, et cetera.

I am declaring war on hopelessness, and I am asking you to join me in the fight against it. Each one of us who makes a commitment to spreading hope everywhere we go will become part of the answer the world needs.

CHAPTER 6

Look Up

I will lift up my eyes to the hills—from whence comes
my help? My help comes from the Lord, Who made heaven
and earth.

Psalm 121:1–2 (NKJV)

Hope is the thing with feathers
That perches in the soul
And sings the tune without the words
And never stops at all.

—Emily Dickinson

One of the things I like to do when I have rest time is watch movies. Dave and I spend so much time traveling that when I get home, I look forward to sitting back in my recliner with my dog in my lap and enjoying a couple of hours relaxing in front of an entertaining movie. You're probably the same way—there's just something enjoyable about a watching a really good movie.

No matter what kind of movies you like to watch (I like the classics or a good mystery), we've all witnessed the same scene. It's a Hollywood favorite that finds its way into action movies, adventure movies, crime thrillers, war movies, and even romantic comedies. I'm talking about the "fear of heights" scene. You've seen it, right? The settings are different but the dilemma is the same—HEIGHTS! The main character is standing on tiptoe out on a narrow ledge, or hesitantly crossing a rickety bridge, or nervously climbing a city tower. Disaster seems unavoidable. In each of these scenes, our hero is ridiculously high up, the wind is blowing, his foot slips once or twice, the music swells…and I'm so nervous I can barely watch!

If you've seen this scene played out as many times as I have, you know there is a classic line that someone seems to always proclaim in this situation. Right as the character, or characters, are walking across the narrowest part of the ledge, traversing the shakiest section of the bridge, or climbing the most dangerous face of the mountain, someone says these words: "Whatever you do, don't look down!" Seems like good advice, doesn't it? Just stay focused, look at where you're going, keep moving, and *don't look down*. But for some reason, our favorite movie characters rarely listen. It's pretty predictable. The first thing they do is look down, and the result is always the same: panic.

Maybe you can relate today. Of course, you're not thousands of feet above the ground right now (at least I hope you're not), but maybe you're on a ledge of financial struggle and it feels as if you're about to slip. Maybe you're in a relationship that is swaying and shaking like a rickety bridge, and you feel it might collapse at any moment. Maybe you're trying to climb over an obstacle so high that it has you nervous and afraid. If that's the case— if you're hurting today—I want to give you some familiar advice: Whatever you do, don't look down.

> Whatever you do, don't look down.

I say "don't look down" because a lot of people look to the wrong things when they find themselves in difficult situations. They focus on the size of the problem, the risks that they're facing, the negative things others are saying, the pain of their past, their own unhealthy feelings and emotions, or their fear of failure. But there is no hope in any of those negative things. Those are all things that are "down," and looking to them will not help you make the climb.

The Bible gives us a better option when we're in need of help. Instead of looking down at the things that can't help us, the Word of God tells us to look up—to put our focus on the One who will always help us. Hebrews 12:2 says: "Looking unto Jesus, the author and finisher of our faith…" (NKJV), and Isaiah 45:22 says, "Look to Me and be saved, all the ends of the earth! For I am God, and there is no other." When he was in trouble, David would turn and look to the heavens, because he knew his help came from on high (see Psalm 121:1–2). I want to encourage you to do the same thing. When you're going through something and you're not sure what to do, where to go, or even where to look…just look up. Look for the Lord. He is the One who can help you. He is the One who will rescue you. He is the One who refuses to let you fall. Jesus said to look up, for our redemption draws near (see Luke 21:28). Our redemption is not in looking down. We look up to God expecting Him to redeem us.

> *When you're going through something and you're not sure what to do, where to go, or even where to look… just look up.*

The phrase "look up" means more than just gaze at the sky. It means to have a hopeful attitude, a positive outlook, and an expectation of something good. God is good, and He is always planning something good for us.

Nothing Can Take God's Place

We often look to people or things during times of uncertainty, and that is understandable but usually ineffective. Even though we know we should trust God, and even though we believe He loves us and has a plan for our lives, there's just a natural temptation to grab onto something tangible—something we can see with the natural eye. We can see God, but we must see Him with the eye of faith. We see Him with our hearts, and we should always put our hope in Him.

As I've traveled the world ministering to people, praying with them, and helping them through struggles, I've discovered there are many things people look to when they're hurting before they think to look to God. Here are just a few of the most common examples:

Looking to Friends

It's great to have friends you can talk to and confide in when you're hurting, especially friends who are believers, who will pray with you and encourage you. However, your friends don't have all the answers. Even though they may be well intentioned, they can guide you in the wrong direction if their advice doesn't line up with God's Word. Our friends might feel sorry for us but may be unwilling to be truthful enough to tell us what we need to hear. I recall when Dave told me that I needed to stop feeling sorry for myself. I didn't like it and I got angry with him, but what he said was true and I needed to hear it. Dave loved me enough to give me what I needed instead of what I wanted. I've seen situations in which friends have kept someone stuck in a dysfunction because they were enabling a person instead of telling that person what she really needed to hear.

There is nothing wrong with depending on your friends in tough times, but don't let your friends take the place of God in your life. Go to the Lord first when you're hurting, and seek God's direction in that situation. After you have spent time in the Word and sought the Lord in prayer, then you may want to go to your friends and share with them what you think the Lord is saying. Remember, your friends are human just like you. Their ability to help you is limited. If you rely solely on them, you will end up disappointed.

Looking to a Spouse

One of the things I learned early on in my marriage is that I couldn't depend on Dave to be the source of my happiness—that's God's place. God is the source of our joy (see Psalm 43:4), not our spouses.

I remember there were times when I would get so upset with Dave because he would go golfing or watch a ball game rather than spend the morning with me. It wasn't like Dave was neglecting me—he's a great husband and he loves to spend time with me—but I wanted him there all the time. I was upset because I was looking to him to be my source of happiness and contentment. I wanted him to make me feel secure and confident. But the Lord showed me that anytime we look to a person (even our spouse) to do what only God can do, we are going to be frustrated in life.

The moment I stopped trying to force Dave to give me things only God could give me, I immediately had a new peace and joy in my life…and in my marriage. With that said, if I'm upset about something or if I need to talk, Dave is always there to encourage and help me, but he and I both know it's only God who can provide everything we need in every situation.

Looking to Yourself

When things get tough in life, there is a tendency in all of us to say "I'll just take care of this myself." Sometimes it's because no one was around to help you when you were younger, so you've always had to be independent. Other times it's because you are a strong person, perhaps very talented, and it's just easier to trust those abilities to get you out of a jam.

But you weren't meant to go through life alone, and there are going to be times when your own strengths aren't going to be enough. You're going to face situations where only God is strong enough to carry you through. I suggest you get used to looking to Him now. Don't wait for an obstacle so big, or a pain so deep, to drive you to Him out of desperation. Get into the habit of waking up every day and saying "Lord, today I trust You. Thank You for the

> *You're going to face situations where only God is strong enough to carry you through.*

gifts and abilities You've given me, but I don't depend on my own understanding. I depend on You. Give me the wisdom, direction, and grace I need today to live an overcoming, victorious life."

As great as friends can be, as wonderful as a godly spouse is, as important as it is to recognize the gifts and talents God has given you, none of these things can take God's place in your life. Psalm 37:39 says: "But the salvation of the [consistently] righteous is of the Lord; He is their Refuge and secure Stronghold in the time of trouble." The Lord is our refuge and our stronghold, no one else. This is why we're filled with hope when we look to the Lord in times of trouble, not people.

Has someone disappointed or let you down? Did it make you angry or resentful? Have you ever considered that perhaps it was your own fault for looking to that person to meet your needs instead of looking to God? I don't mean that to sound harsh, or as if I don't empathize with your pain, but the truth that we need to hear is often painful initially. If we have more of our hope and confidence in people than we do in God, He will reveal their weaknesses and let them disappoint us so we will eventually turn to Him. It may not feel good right now, but truth will make us free!

Ignore the Storm—Focus on Jesus

Matthew 14:24–33 paints a pretty dramatic picture. The disciples are trying to sail across the Sea of Galilee at night when a ferocious storm arises. Now, if any individuals could handle themselves in a ship during a storm, it was Peter and the disciples. After all, these men were experienced fishermen. This wasn't their first storm. But the strength of this storm exceeded their experience.

Have you ever found yourself in a situation like that? Have you ever thought you could handle a situation, only to realize that this storm was different from the others? Well, this is exactly what happened to the disciples; this was a storm they couldn't rescue themselves from.

Seeing that the disciples needed help, Jesus "came to them, walking on the sea" (v. 25). I love how nonchalantly the Bible records that. There's no bold type; it's not in all capital letters; the sentence doesn't even have an exclamation mark. Jesus was walking on the water, and we shouldn't be surprised. It's as if God is telling us He can and will do whatever it takes to get to us when we're hurting. There is no storm big enough to keep God from rescuing you.

> There is no storm big enough to keep God from rescuing you.

When Jesus came to the boat, the disciples were afraid. They thought Jesus was a ghost. But Peter said, "Lord, if it is You, command me to come to You on the water" (v. 28). As soon as Jesus said "Come," Peter got out of the boat and, miraculously, he began to walk on the water. Peter didn't do this in his own strength (he certainly didn't have the power to walk on water), and Peter didn't do this with the help of the other disciples (they didn't give him the advice necessary for taking a stroll on the waves). It was only the Lord who could do this. Jesus was Peter's only hope.

As Peter was walking toward Jesus, he did what you and I often do—he took his eyes off the Lord and looked down. He looked at the waves and started focusing on the storm. Instead of thinking *I'm walking on the water with Jesus! This is amazing! There is no limit to what God can do in my life!*—Peter started thinking *What if I drown? How is this even possible? Can Jesus really rescue me?* That's what happens when you look down at your problems instead of up at your promise. Exclamation marks turn into question marks. Faith turns into fear. And you begin to sink. Thankfully, we have a Savior who helps us even when our faith is weak. Jesus reached out and rescued Peter. It wasn't the disciples who rescued him, it was Jesus.

This story perfectly illustrates what happens in the storms of your life. It doesn't matter how big the storm, it's not too big for God. He sees you, exactly where you are, and He is coming to your rescue. If you're experiencing a struggle today, start looking for God. Don't be like the disciples who were surprised when Jesus showed up; instead, have a happy anticipation that God is going to show up on the scene, that He won't be late, and that He is going to calm the storm. As long as you look to Him, you can walk above the things that threaten to destroy your life. You can live with peace, joy, contentment, and happiness because you're focused on Jesus. But the

> *Have a happy anticipation that God is going to show up on the scene, that He won't be late, and that He is going to calm the storm.*

moment you begin to look at the waves—the negative reports, the fearful thoughts, what others think, lies from the enemy—these are the things that will sink you every time. Even in the midst of a chaotic storm, when it feels like everything is shaking in your life, look to the Lord. He is the only thing that cannot be shaken.

The One Thing You Can Always Depend On

God wants you to be full of hope, not full of discouragement, despair, and depression. The Bible tells us in Romans 5:5 that those who put their hope in God will never be disappointed and they will never be put to shame. Wow! Think about that. You may put your hope in friends and get disappointed. You may put your hope in your bank account and be disappointed. You may put your hope in a politician and be disappointed. You may put your hope in a job and be disappointed. But if you put your hope in God, you won't be disappointed. Even though you may go through things you don't understand at times, He will always work them all out for good in the end.

As long as you've got hope, you've got possibility, because everything is subject to change except for God. It doesn't matter what kind of a bad report you get, the first thing you ought to think is *Well, that's subject to change.* Your finances change, your children change, your boss changes, your situation changes, but God doesn't. God is a rock—He is constant. Malachi 3:6 says, "For I am the Lord, I do not change." People change, the weather changes, circumstances change, minds can change, moods can change, commitments change, jobs change, schools change. This is something we might as well get used to. The only thing we can be sure of in this world is that something is always going to be changing. That's why it is so important to keep your hope in the Lord and build your life on the Rock. As long as you make God the main source of all that you need— knowing that He is the only One who never changes—you can handle anything else that does change because God is your foundation in life.

We suffer a great deal emotionally that we really wouldn't have to endure if we would put our hope in God and stop expecting someone else to do what only God can do.

Get Your Hopes Up!

Every day is not a perfect day, and every storm is not in the forecast. We may have a headache or a heartache. It may last a day or it may last longer. But whatever the struggle you may be facing, I want to encourage you to LOOK UP! Don't focus on the negative circumstances, the odds stacked against you, or the fearful thoughts that arise.

When you look up, hope is reborn. Even though the storm may be great, it's not greater than God. All you have to do is look for Him and trust that He'll do whatever it takes—even walk on water—to get to you. So go ahead and get your hopes up. You're going to come through this stronger than before. Just stay focused on Jesus, have a positive attitude, keep moving, and, whatever you do . . . don't look down.

CHAPTER 7

Count Your Blessings Instead of Your Problems

Praise the Lord, my soul, and forget not all his benefits…
Psalm 103:2 (NIV)

"Only in the darkness can you see the stars."
—Martin Luther King Jr.

I once heard a story about a man who lost his keys one evening. Desperate to find them, he searched frantically outside on the corner of the street, directly under the streetlight. A passerby noticed his frenzied search and stopped to help him look for the missing keys. After a few minutes of diligent searching, the helpful stranger asked, "Now, where was it exactly that you dropped your keys? If we know the spot, maybe we'll have better luck." Without hesitation, the owner of the lost keys answered, "I dropped them when I was in my house." Dumbfounded at this reply, the helpful stranger exclaimed, "If you dropped them in your house, why are we looking out here under this streetlight?" The owner of the lost keys responded, "Because the light is better out here."

Your first thought is probably *That is ridiculous. Anybody knows better than to do that.* It may sound silly to be looking for the keys you lost in your house while standing under a streetlight, but I tell you that story for a reason. Many times in life, we're searching for something we need, but we're searching in the wrong places. There's an old song that says we're "looking for love in all the wrong places." I think that's true. But I also think we often look for hope in all the wrong places.

If we really want to enjoy life, we are going to have to make a basic change in where we look for hope. Jesus must be the source of our hope at all times. It doesn't matter what the circumstances are around us. Our circumstances shouldn't be the things that determine our level of joy. Even if we are having the worst day ever, we can have a confident, joy-filled, hopeful attitude if we learn to look at what we have left, not what we have lost. Always look at what God is doing, not what you think He isn't doing.

> Look at what we have left, not what we have lost.

I wish someone had shared that truth with me earlier in life. For many years I was a miserable, frustrated Christian, and one of the main reasons was because I was always thinking about what I didn't have. And I didn't just think about it; I complained about it. I would spend my prayer time telling the Lord all the things I didn't have. *God, I don't have enough money. I don't have the same talent as someone else. I didn't have a good childhood.* The list goes on and on. I looked around me and did a daily inventory of everything I did not have.

But the Lord began to show me that I had a lot, I was just looking in the wrong places. There is no victory in focusing on the things you lost or don't have. Instead of putting my energy and effort into complaining about what I had lost, the Lord began to teach me to focus on what I had left. I may not have had the money to go on a fancy vacation, but at least I had the money to pay my bills that month. I may not have had an ability that someone else had, but I was a good communicator, and eventually God began to use that to help people. I may have been abused as a child, but God was healing me. My husband and my children were not perfect, but I was blessed with a family. My mother and father had forsaken me, but the Lord had adopted me (see Psalm 27:10).

The more I began to focus on what I had left rather than what I had lost, the more my attitude began to change. I began to see God's blessings and His favor on my life, and my hope began to soar.

The same can be true for you. No matter what you are going through today, you can discover a new joy in life. You may have lost some things; there may be some advantages you don't have. But instead of focusing on what you have lost, why don't you search through what you have left? You just might be surprised at what you find.

Three Pennies and God

I once read that when Mother Teresa began her missions work in India, she had no money. She had a dream to build an orphanage and to help the people of Calcutta, but the funds weren't there. When asked how much money she actually had, she said, "Three pennies." People doubted her mission, asking "What can you do with only three pennies?" But Mother Teresa replied, "I have three pennies and God, what else do I need?"

I love this attitude. Mother Teresa wasn't concerned about only having three pennies because she had God! I wonder how our lives would change if we started counting up exactly what God has given us. It might not seem like much if we compare it to what others have, and it might not even seem like much compared to what we are praying for, but even a little bit is all God needs. Three pennies is more than enough in the hands of God. If God can feed a crowd of 5,000 men (plus women and children) with just a few loaves of bread and a couple of fish, just think about what He can do with the little bit you have. You may think *But I don't have anything, not*

> Three pennies is more than enough in the hands of God.

even three pennies. You can still be encouraged because God created the entire Universe out of nothing. He started by speaking words of faith over an empty void. No matter how little we have, we can all do that.

Have you ever been in a grocery store when they are doing stock inventory? It's amazing to watch the entire team of inventory employees come in and start counting what's in the store. They pull out their hand-held devices, they label every item, then they meticulously count and recount to make sure they get the numbers right. The thing that amazes me is nothing is overlooked. They count even the smallest things. Every pack of gum, every dented can, every bruised banana—a complete inventory counts it all.

I think it would be a great idea if we took an inventory of our own lives and counted every blessing God has given us. That would increase our hope and build our faith. Instead of moping around talking about what we don't have yet, we can walk in confidence thanking God for everything He has given

> *I think it would be a great idea if we took an inventory of our own lives and counted every blessing God has given us.*

us. And we should count every single thing. It may appear small, but count it anyway and thank Him for it. Form a habit of noticing everything God does for you, and the more you meditate on His blessings, the more your hope will abound. God has given us Jesus, and if He has done that, will He not also give us all other things?

Inventory Time

Everybody's inventory list is going to look different. We don't all have the same gifts, talents, strengths, or provisions—and we certainly don't all have them at the same time—but God never promised you would have what someone else has or that person would have what you have. I recall being in a leper colony during a visit to India, and a man with leprosy asked me if I would like to see his home. He seemed very excited, so I gladly went with him to take a look. It turned out that what he was calling home was a hole about 10 feet long and 6 feet high dug out of the side of a dirt hill. It was furnished with a home-made hammock, a couple of dented pots, and a few dishes. I must admit I was convicted to the core when I realized how happy he was with so little and how unhappy I often am with so much.

With that in mind, here is a list of suggested things to thank God for. You may not have everything on this list (right now), but maybe many of them will resonate with you. The leper I met would have been elated to have any of these things.

- A roof over your head
- A friend who checks in on you
- Family members who love you
- A car that is running (yes, even if it's barely running)
- A full stomach
- Hot and cold running water
- A sense of humor
- A weekly paycheck
- A comfortable bed
- A dream in your heart
- Educational opportunities for your children
- A local church that encourages you
- A healthy body
- A closet full of clothes
- A Bible to read
- Hope for the future

And those are just a few things that came to my mind. I bet if you took the time to think and pray about it, you could come up with a list 10 times longer than this one.

Some of those things I mentioned may seem pretty basic, but if you think about it, there are people around the world who don't have even the most basic things you have. Water, food, shelter—these things aren't to be taken for granted. We should be thanking God for these basic necessities and never for a minute take them for granted.

There's Always Hope

An inventory of God's goodness is important, because, to be honest, it's easy to look at the struggles in life and get discouraged. If we just look at the obstacles, it's easy to lose hope. You might look at your bank account and feel hopeless. Sometimes you might look at your kids and want to throw your hands up in the air and say "There's no hope." You may look at yourself and say the same thing! You may drive to work thinking *There's no hope.* That is exactly what the devil wants you to do. He knows if he can keep us hopeless, we cannot move on to bold faith and we will miss God's good plan for us.

Resist the temptation to look at what you have lost or don't have and choose to look at all that God has done, is doing, and will do. When you do, hope will come alive, joy will increase, faith will grow, and activity will increase. Remember that when you live in the garden of hope, something is always blooming.

Instead of saying "There's no hope," why not say "There's always hope!" Decide to take an inventory of what God has given you and choose to hope for more. Make a list of the blessings God has given you, and perhaps read them out loud each day. The more you focus on what you have, the more amazed you will be at God's goodness in your life.

> *Instead of saying "There's no hope," why not say "There's always hope!"*

Ephesians 1:3 (NIV) says:

> *Praise be to the God and Father of our Lord Jesus Christ, who*
> *has blessed us in the heavenly realms with every spiritual*
> *blessing in Christ.*

That should give you hope. No matter what you are facing today, you are going to be blessed with everything you'll ever need. If you need strength, if you need faith, if you need hope, if you need a friend, if you need understanding, if you need peace or joy or righteousness, or money, or health, or healing, or victory, God is going to provide it for you. Philippians 4:19 says: "And my God will liberally supply (fill to the full) your every need according to His riches in glory in Christ Jesus."

In the times when you may doubt that God is actually going to provide those things in the present or in the future, just look back at what He has already done. Look back at your inventory of blessings and let it boost your faith for the future. That's what David did. When King Saul and David's brothers doubted whether David could actually defeat Goliath, David just stopped and took an inventory of the goodness of God in his life. He said, "Your servant killed both the lion and the bear; and this uncircumcised Philistine shall be like one of them, for he has defied the armies of the living God!" (1 Samuel 17:36). David was confident that, because God had done those things for him in the past, God would do even greater things in the present situation. David's inventory of blessings gave him the hope he needed to live out his destiny.

Blessing You Is Something God Loves to Do

More than anything, when you start taking an inventory of God's goodness in your life—when you start to count your blessings—it fills your heart with joy. I've noticed it's impossible to be thankful and discouraged at the same time. It doesn't work. If you'll take a moment each day to focus on God's blessings and His favor, you won't be able to help it...you'll be filled to overflowing with the joy of the Lord.

> I've noticed it's impossible to be thankful and discouraged at the same time.

The Word of God tells us the joy of the Lord is our strength (see Nehemiah 8:10). Many people are lethargic, feeling tired, and barely making it from the chair at their desk at work to the couch at home because of a joyless attitude. Some people are completely worn-out when they come home from work, and it's not because of their jobs—it's because they've got a bad attitude about the places they work and all the people there. A negative attitude will affect every part of our lives—even our health. But if we decide to be happy about what God has given us and focus on the good in life, we will not only be happier, but we will be healthier.

Every day I keep a journal during my time with the Lord. I write down Scripture verses that encourage me, some of the prayer requests I'm praying that day, things I feel like the Lord is putting on my heart, and special things that God does for me. I have years and years' worth of these journals that I've saved, and from time to time, I like to read through them. When I thumb through the past journals, it's interesting to me that several times a year, God reminds me to have an aggressive expectation of good. It must be really important. When I'm full of hope—when I'm expecting God to do something great in my life—it builds my spirit and fills me with joy. I take vitamins regularly, and I think that hope is the "happy vitamin." We should take hope in large doses daily! I think that's why one of my favorite Scripture verses is:

> And therefore the Lord [earnestly] waits [expecting, looking, and longing] to be gracious to you; and therefore He lifts Himself up, that He may have mercy on you and show

loving-kindness to you. For the Lord is a God of justice. Blessed (happy, fortunate, to be envied) are all those who [earnestly] wait for Him, who expect and look and long for Him [for His victory, His favor, His love, His peace, His joy, and His matchless, unbroken companionship]!

Isaiah 30:18

> God is actually "expecting, looking, and longing" to show you His goodness. This is why you can have a happy expectation of good in your life.

God is actually "expecting, looking, and longing" to show you His goodness. This is why you can have a happy expectation of good in your life. This isn't something God is begrudgingly agreeing to do—this is something He loves to do. Jesus died for you so that you may "have and enjoy life, and have it in abundance" (John 10:10). So don't go through life with a bad attitude. Decide to have a good attitude, expecting good things from the Lord. We don't expect them because we deserve them, but because God is good! Choose to praise God with a thankful heart for all the things He has given you.

Get Your Hopes Up!

As you finish this chapter, ask yourself *How hopeful am I?* Are you excited each day, expecting that God is going to answer a prayer, fulfill a dream, meet a need, and do something amazing in your life? If you're not as hopeful as you'd like to be, you can change that. It's not a complicated process—it all begins with looking at what you have left instead of what you have lost.

Take an inventory of the blessings in your life. Many of the things on your list will be large things that are clearly obvious, but many of the things on your list will be small things too. Make sure you take the time to really look at every part of your life and see the little, overlooked things that God has been blessing you with all along. When you do, you're going to notice a total shift in the way you view your life. Your marriage, your family, your career, your aspirations—your view of it all changes when you have a grateful heart.

So go ahead and get your hopes up today. God has blessed you in the past—you've got an entire list to prove it—and that's just the beginning. He has more in store for you. Just make sure you're looking for it in the right places.

CHAPTER 8

Words of Hope

Why are you cast down, O my inner self? And why should
you moan over me and be disquieted within me? Hope in
God and wait expectantly for Him, for I shall yet praise Him,
Who is the help of my [sad] countenance, and my God.

Psalm 43:5

"Hope smiles from the threshold of the year to come,
whispering 'it will be happier'..."

—Alfred, Lord Tennyson

In the same way that the food we eat affects us physically, the words
we speak affect us spiritually, mentally, and emotionally. I believe
that they also affect us physically, because the more full of hope
and happiness our conversation is, the more energetic we feel. A
positive, hopeful attitude relieves stress, which is the root cause of a
lot of sickness and disease.

Several years ago, I decided to get serious about my health. I was
lacking energy, getting sick easily, and dealing with nagging physical problems. In the past, I had attempted different diets and work-
out plans, but my work always crowded out any time I had to take
care of myself. I would end up back at my normal busy pace, even
though I knew it wasn't good for me. Eventually, I decided enough
was enough. I guess you could say I got tired of being tired.

One of the first things I began to realize as I studied proper diet and exercise routines is that everything we eat affects our body's performance. We all know that a healthy diet is important, but I don't think we always realize just how much our nutritional choices really impact our bodies. What you eat on any given day can determine how you feel, how much you get accomplished, and what kind of attitude you're going to have. Good or bad—salad or doughnuts—the food that goes into your mouth affects your body. It can also affect your emotions and your thought processes.

In the same way—hopeful declarations or negative confessions—the words you speak affect your life in many ways. Words have power. What you say makes a difference. As soon as you say something, those words go into your ears and directly to your soul. If your words are filled with life, you will feel happier and more energetic. However, if you have a tendency to talk about what is wrong in life and complain about your situation, those words have a negative impact and will drain your energy and make you feel discouraged and even depressed. Don't put hope off until another time because "hope deferred makes the heart sick" (see Proverbs 13:12).

Words filled with hope are important, especially when you are facing something difficult. One of the most important things you can do when you're hurting is speak positive, faith-filled words. I'm not saying that your words alone have the power to change the situation—only God can do that—but your words do have power in the spiritual realm, and when you agree with God, His plan can rapidly begin to come to pass in your life. Your words can change your attitude about a negative situation and help determine how quickly you overcome it. The Israelites complained while they were in the wilderness, and they remained there. An 11-day journey took 40 years, and most of them never arrived at their desired destination.

Complaining and rehearsing everything we think is wrong in our

> *One of the most important things you can do when you're hurting is speak positive, faith-filled words.*

life is a greater problem than most people realize it is. It is evil in the Lord's ears! I wonder how many people go through life complaining, and by doing so, never have the kind of life they wish they had. You see, wishing is not enough to bring good things to pass. We need living hope and strong faith in God. We also need power thoughts and words filled with hope. We need action when it is called for and a thankful heart while we are waiting.

I spent the first 45 years of my life damaging my days and hindering my future through lack of knowledge about the power of my own words. I lacked knowledge in many areas, but this was a big one for me. If you are educated about word power, this chapter will merely serve as a refresher course that will keep you going in the right direction, but if this is all new to you, it can be absolutely life-changing.

You may not realize that you are in charge of your words. You can choose what you will say, and believe me when I tell you that what you say matters a great deal. Be a good steward of words! Choose them wisely and believe what God's Word says concerning them being filled with the power of life or death.

> *Death and life are in the power of the tongue, and they who*
> *indulge in it shall eat the fruit of it [for death or life].*
>
> Proverbs 18:21

Stop Talking About Your Problems

Have you ever noticed that Jesus didn't talk about His problems? He could have; He had to deal with a lot of the same things you and I have to deal with. Jesus had a hectic schedule. Jesus encountered rude and obnoxious people. Jesus faced tough situations. Not to mention the fact that He knew He was going to suffer terribly and die on the cross for the sins of the world.

But when you read the Gospels, you never hear Jesus saying anything critical or that could be defined as complaining or murmuring.

He obviously knew the power of words. When the time for His suffering and death was near, He told His disciples that He would not be
talking with them much from now on (see John 14:30). Why would
He say that? It was because He knew the power of words, and He also
knew how tempting it is to say all the wrong things when we are going
through difficult or painful times. He knew that His Father had a plan
for the salvation of man and that it hinged on Him, and He was determined to do everything necessary to stay in agreement with God,
including speaking words that God could use, not ones that the devil
could use.

> *I will not talk with you much more, for the prince (evil genius,*
> *ruler) of the world is coming. And he has no claim on Me. [He*
> *has nothing in common with Me; there is nothing in Me that*
> *belongs to him, and he has no power over Me.]*
>   *But [Satan is coming and] I do as the Father has com-*
> *manded Me, so that the world may know (be convinced)*
> *that I love the Father and that I do only what the Father has*
> *instructed Me to do. [I act in full agreement with His orders.]*
> *Rise, let us go away from here.*

John 14:30–31

Of course, Jesus talked about many things, including sin. There
were times when Jesus scolded the Pharisees and corrected His disciples. As you read the Gospels, you find that Jesus talked about
a lot of things, but His problems weren't one of them. Luke 4:22
says that the people "marveled at the words of grace that came forth
from His mouth." Jesus was on a mission, and He wasn't about to get
sidelined by focusing on the everyday problems of life. He said that
His words were spirit and life (see John 6:63).

Are your words spirit and life, or carnal (fleshly) and death? The
good news is that you can make a change right now if you need to. I
am the first to admit that the mouth is impossible to control without

a lot of help from God. However, if we make the right decision and come into agreement with God's will in this area, He will certainly help us make positive changes.

Take the Narrow Path

Jesus instructs us to take the narrow path that leads to life and to avoid the broad path that leads to destruction (see Matthew 7:13–14). Obviously, the narrow path is more difficult to walk on. I always say that on the narrow path there is no room for our carnal, fleshly ways. We can go through life saying what we feel like saying and having no regard for the power of our words, but that puts us on the broad path that Jesus said leads to destruction, and I doubt that any of us want that.

It's easy to get focused on the things that aren't going right. It seems like so many of our conversations are focused on what's going wrong rather than what's going right. They are not hope-full, they are hope-less! *The kids are sick. The traffic is terrible. My feet hurt. The economy is down. Can you believe what she said about me? I can't afford that.* But the more we talk about what's going wrong, the more power we give it in our life.

Have you ever considered that you might be making your problems worse by talking about them excessively? Have you ever considered that you might not be making progress in life due to complaining? I certainly had not considered these things until the Holy Spirit confronted me about them, and I am so glad that He did because we can't change any area of our lives where we lack knowledge.

> When you're going through a trying time, the best thing you can do is stop talking about how big your problem is and start talking about how big God is.

When you're going through a trying time, the best thing you can do is stop talking about how big your problem is and start talking about how big God is. Take some time each day to meditate on God's Word and speak His promises over your situation. Power comes pouring in when you focus on what can happen with God on your side instead of what is happening in your life right now.

Doing What Is Right on Purpose

You may not always feel positive, and you may not always want to speak positive words. There are going to be days when you wake up feeling downright terrible. These are the days when it is really easy to be bitter, to complain, to have a pessimistic view of life. But you don't have to live subject to your feelings. Feelings are fickle—they change quickly depending on any number of factors.

One of the main points I want to make in this book is that we are to hope on purpose. We cannot sit around and wish we felt it, or even just pray we had it. We choose to be "hope-full" (full of hope) each day. One of the most amazing things about having free will is that we can choose our attitudes, thoughts, words, and actions. I am sure, if you are like me, the first thing you like to think when you have done the wrong thing is *I just can't help it*, and then that is followed with some sort of excuse for why you didn't do right.

It might play out like this: *I wish I felt hopeful, but I just don't have anything very happy going on in my life. I can't be expected to have a positive outlook when all I see is trouble everywhere I look. If I had the advantages a lot of people do, then my attitude would be better.* But it could be like this: *My circumstances are not very good right now, but I choose to be full of hope. I am expecting something good to happen in my life today! Yes, something good is going to happen to me and through me!*

Doing this on purpose on a daily basis even when you don't feel like it will ultimately change the way you feel. Your feelings will bow to your decisions in due time. No matter how circumstances look, any day with Jesus is better than any day without Him. We can always be hopeful because He loves us, He is for us, and He can change anything! He is a God of justice, and He makes wrong things right!

On days when you feel discouraged, decide you're not going to let those feelings control your life. Instead of having a negative outlook and speaking negative words, make declarations that are in agreement with God's Word!

- I know that God loves me (see Ephesians 3:19).
- I believe I will see the Lord's goodness in my life (see Psalm 27:13).
- I am more than a conqueror through Christ who loves me (see Romans 8:37).

I've been preaching almost 40 years, and I still meditate on and declare God's Word almost every day of my life. No matter what I feel like, I remind myself who I am in Christ—and you can do the same thing. Don't wait for somebody else to cheer you up; stir yourself up in the Lord.

> Don't wait for somebody else to cheer you up; stir yourself up in the Lord.

I like to think of this as a little personal pep rally. If you ever attended a pep rally in middle school or high school, you know what I'm talking about. A pep rally is when the cheerleaders cheer, the band plays, and the student body gets ready for the big game. A pep rally is a celebration based on an expected victory. Even though the team hasn't won yet, the cheering has already begun.

Well, you certainly have something to cheer about in your life. No matter what opposition you are facing, God is on your side, and He is undefeated. So go ahead and have a pep rally—get excited about the victory God is bringing in your life.

The Hope Found in Praise

2 Chronicles chapter 20 tells the story of a large army that came against King Jehoshaphat and the army of Judah. The people were

afraid because they knew they were vastly outnumbered (see 2 Chronicles 20:15). Have you ever felt that way, or do you perhaps feel that way now? Do you feel that your problems are simply too great for you to ever come out the winner?

Jehoshaphat was informed that the battle wasn't his but God's. Armed with that word from the Lord, Jehoshaphat prepared his army for battle. But he did something much different for this battle. Instead of lining up his fiercest warriors at the front of the battle lines as everyone expected him to do, Jehoshaphat gave that position to the worshippers. 2 Chronicles 20:21 says:

> *...He appointed singers to sing to the Lord and praise Him in their holy [priestly] garments as they went out before the army, saying, Give thanks to the Lord, for His mercy and loving-kindness endure forever!*

Jehoshaphat began the battle with praise. What a picture that must have been—an entire army marching out for battle under the banner of praise.

The Bible says in verse 22 that as "they began to sing and to praise," God confused the enemy armies. Instead of fighting against Judah, these people turned against each other in confusion. By the time Jehoshaphat and his army arrived on the scene, the enemy was destroyed. God had won the battle just as He promised.

I believe the devil gets confused when we praise God in the midst of times when we should be fearful and complaining. Praise and thanksgiving actually defeat him.

Praise is a powerful weapon. It declares that you trust God and are completely depending on Him. Don't wait for your circumstance to change before you speak words of hope. Let me be as plain as I can be: No matter what is happening in your life right now, don't let any sickness, or problem, or loss, or fear of impending trouble keep you from praising God. Choose your words carefully, open your mouth, and boldly declare that God is faithful and you are expecting something good to happen in your life.

Romans 4:20 says Abraham "grew strong and was empowered by faith as he gave praise and glory to God." The same thing happens in your life when you speak words of praise—you grow strong and you are empowered by faith to overcome every obstacle you may be facing. Put praise on the front lines of your life!

Say This, Not That

When people are full of hope, they are expecting something good to happen to them, and you can tell by the things they say. They're confident good things will happen in their circumstances, they're excited that change is in the air, they're expecting breakthrough— so that's what they love to talk about. Hopeful people are optimistic and upbeat. They are fun to be around. Hope is contagious! It is one of the best gifts we can give anyone. Why not see yourself as a dispenser of hope? It is one of the things that our society today is desperately in need of. I especially feel empathy for our teens and young adults these days. They need all the encouragement they can get!

The world, our schools, and our universities often convey a message that God is a myth or at best someone who doesn't need to be considered or discussed. The world seems to be trying to tuck God away in a corner, almost as if He is an embarrassment. As a teenager, I remember God being openly talked about in all sectors of society. He was part of everyday conversation. We saw the Ten Commandments on school walls, and public prayer was a common occurrence. My parents were not godly people, but I still heard about God in school and from neighbors. Our youth today don't have that benefit, and it is easy for them to be hopeless.

Many parents are busy trying to make ends meet and have little or no time to spend with their children. Stress in the family often provokes parents to nag their teens about their clothing, the way they style (or don't style) their hair, choices of friends, grades, chores left undone, and countless other things. I certainly believe parents need to correct their children, but perhaps if the children had more hope, they wouldn't need so much correction! If they are not getting it, they leave home each day feeling hopeless before they even face the rest of the world, which will more than likely only add to their hopeless state. Speak uplifting, encouraging, and hope-filled words to everyone and especially to our youth today.

Make up your mind that you are going to be a chatterbox of hope. Decide that you are going to be a positive influence in the world. Be a person other people want to be around. Live your life

> Make up your mind that you are going to be a chatterbox of hope.

with the belief and hope that something good is going to happen today.

Get Your Hopes Up!

What you say today goes a long way in determining the life you are going to live tomorrow. Don't allow the pressures of the world and the lies of the enemy to discourage you, causing you to see only the negative things in life. Look to the Word of God, stand on His promises, and speak life to your situation.

Every word you say affects you, so choose to speak healthy, life-giving words. Let those words pave the way as you walk through every difficult situation. Instead of talking about your problems, start talking about God's promises, and let those declarations of hope stir up your faith.

Go ahead and get your hopes up today. Even if you feel weak, even if it seems impossible, even if a battle has you feeling unsure and afraid, put praise on the front lines. When you do, you'll realize God is fighting for you—there's no way you can lose.

CHAPTER 9

Keep Moving

Not only so, but we also glory in our sufferings, because we know that suffering produces perseverance; perseverance, character; and character, hope.

Romans 5:3–4 (NIV)

"The greatest glory in living lies not in never falling, but in rising every time we fall."

—Nelson Mandela

Different animals have different instincts when threatened or dealing with fear. Bears attack, squirrels climb, antelope run, and moles dig. All of these instinctual responses are active. But there is one animal whose reaction is quite different: the possum. The possum is an animal that doesn't charge, climb, flee, or dig. The possum just freezes. Rather than getting active, it gets passive. It plays dead—which is where we get the term "playing possum"—and it hopes that staying still will accomplish something.

I've noticed that many times when people are hurt or frightened, they become spiritual possums. Rather than getting active, they get passive. When times get tough, when they're dealing with pain or disappointment, they freeze. They just stop moving. Does this sound familiar? Have you ever found yourself in a holding pattern because of an unexpected trial or a crushing disappointment? Have you ever been in a situation where you don't know what to do, so you do nothing?

If you've dealt with a hurt that has you frozen in your tracks, I'm not making light of your pain. Trust me; I've gone through plenty of trying times that have hurt so badly I felt like I couldn't keep going. I understand what you're going through, because I too have felt paralyzed by a hardship. But I do want to encourage you in the midst of your pain that sometimes the very best thing you can do is just keep moving.

> *Sometimes the very best thing you can do is just keep moving.*

You may not have all the answers yet. You may still be shocked by the circumstances. You may even feel like the world is caving in around you. But in the midst of those difficulties, if you'll just keep moving, it will help you not to become hopeless. You may not be able to see a light at the end of the tunnel right now, but if you'll cast your cares on the Lord and trust that He is with you in this hardship, you'll discover healing as you walk with Him. Eventually, not only will you find the light at the end of the tunnel, the light will chase away every dark thing in your life.

I understand that, depending on the severity of the situation you are facing, there are going to be some days when you won't feel like doing anything. With severe loss comes a natural grieving process that consists of different stages. But as you move through the healing process, just know that the final answer isn't to isolate yourself and spend your life immobilized by pain. God wants you to keep taking steps of faith, trusting that He is going to bring you through the hurt and into something better.

> *The steps of a [good] man are directed and established by the Lord. . . . Though he falls, he shall not be utterly cast down, for the Lord grasps his hand in support and upholds him.*
>
> Psalm 37:23–24

The privilege of trusting God is absolutely wonderful. It allows us to have hope when there seems to be no reason to hope. When all seems lost, you can trust God to direct your steps.

I just heard from a friend who has gone through a terrible ordeal with cancer. She is at the end of her treatments now and ready to reenter daily life. She said, "I am having difficulty knowing how to go forward since my life will not ever be the same as it was." You may relate to this quite well. Perhaps a loved one has died and you can't imagine life without that person. You may have lost a job you worked at for many years and assumed you would retire from. What now? Be assured that even though you don't know, God does. He will guide your every step.

The Power of Pressing On

I remember receiving some devastating news right before I had to begin a three-day conference. It was difficult to keep moving, but I knew that I had to. I sensed the Holy Spirit saying "Just keep putting one foot in front of the other. Keep moving!"

Continuing to move didn't take away all the pain and disappointment I felt, but it did keep me from sinking into a pit of despair, and within a few weeks, the situation was resolved. One of the symptoms of spiritual maturity is having the discipline to keep your commitments, even while you're going through very difficult times. I was hurting, but I needed to continue ministering to others who were hurting, and as I did, God healed me and solved my problem.

As difficult as it is to remember when we are hurting, things do pass and come to an end. Spring always comes after winter. The sun shines again after the storm. Yesterday it was cloudy all day, and eventually we had thunderstorms and heavy rain, but today the sky is blue and the sun is shining. I think we can see, even in the natural weather patterns and seasonal changes, how bad things always give way to good things. If it is cloudy and storming in your life today, look forward to the sun that will probably be shining tomorrow, or the next day or the one after that. It won't storm forever!

> It won't storm forever!

The Bible gives us an example of a sick woman (the woman with the issue of blood) who had to *press through* the crowd to get to Jesus (see Mark 5:25–34; Luke 8:43–48). Even though this woman had been sick 12 years and spent all she had on doctors who were unable to help her, she refused to sit back, passively waiting for her pain to go away. She chose to let hope inspire her to press through every adversity. Nothing was going to keep her from Jesus—not the crowd, not the sickness, not how long she had waited, not her doubts, not her pain. She kept saying to herself *If I could only touch the hem of His garment, I know I shall be made whole* (see Matthew 9:21). With hope and faith in her heart, she just kept moving.

You may have your own crowd to press through today. It may be a crowd of negative thoughts. It may be a crowd of pain and hurt from the past. It may be a crowd of unsupportive people around you. It may be a crowd of financial pressure. It may be a crowd of pain in your body. But if you press past all of those things and refuse to let the disappointments of life keep you stuck in discouragement and misery, your breakthrough will come.

Philippians 3:13–14 says:

> *I do not consider, brethren, that I have captured and made it my own [yet]; but one thing I do [it is my one aspiration]: forgetting what lies behind and straining forward to what lies ahead,* **I press on** *toward the goal to win the [supreme and heavenly] prize to which God in Christ Jesus is calling us upward.* (emphasis added)

I love this passage of Scripture. Paul said that he was going to forget what was behind—the mistakes and pain of his past—and he was going to press forward toward his destiny. You can do the same thing. You can press past all those things that would try to hold you back. Today you can refuse to have a defeated attitude. Today you can refuse to "play possum." You can choose to keep moving—you can choose to press on.

God Is on the Move

You may be reading this and thinking *Joyce, I don't know if I can keep moving. I'm going through something really difficult, and I don't feel like I can take another step.* If this is you today, I urge you not to give in to those feelings. If we are going to follow God, we will need to keep moving in faith. As I study the Word of God, I can't help but notice that God is always moving. Not only that, He is always calling His people to move . . . even in the toughest circumstances.

> When the Israelites left Egypt, and the Egyptian army pursued them, pinning them against the Red Sea . . . *God told them to keep moving!*
>
> After 40 years in the desert, when the children of Israel came to the Jordan River, unsure whether they should cross into Canaan . . . *God told them to keep moving!*
>
> When the army of Israel came up against a fortified Jericho and had no idea how they would win the battle, they were instructed to march around the city. In other words . . . *God told them to keep moving!*
>
> As God's people entered Canaan, finding the land inhabited by giants, God instructed them to conquer the land . . . *God told them to keep moving!*

In all of these situations, the people were tempted to "play possum." The difficulties they were facing made them want to hide and wait rather than get up and get moving. But in each instance, God instructed them to move forward and trust that He would lead them out of trouble and into victory. Had they sat frozen in fear and uncertainty, they never would have experienced the abundance God had for them. Even though it was difficult at the time, they chose to get up and get going. And in the end, it was more than worth it.

The biblical examples aren't just in the Old Testament. As you read the Gospel accounts of the life of Jesus, you see that He was always on the move. He didn't freeze and play spiritual possum every time He faced adversity. He kept moving from one city to another, from one person to another, determined to do what He was on this Earth to do. Even when people didn't accept Him, even when the Pharisees tried to trap Him, even when the crowds turned against Him, Jesus kept moving.

I believe one of the reasons God always kept His children moving—against opposing armies, across rivers, into the Promised Land—is because there is hope in movement. If you're not walking, you have no hope of arriving somewhere new.

Without forward motion, there is no hope of change!

Taking a Step of Obedience

One of the ways you can keep moving is just by being obedient to God—you can simply do what He leads you to do. The steps He asks you to take may be small or big, they may even be unexpected, but following God is the only way we will ever end up at the right destination.

I keep thinking of the Israelites and how the cloud of God's presence led them through the wilderness. The cloud covered the tabernacle, and the Bible says that when the cloud moved, the Israelites journeyed, and when it remained, they remained. They never knew when it was going to move, but they had to be ready to move when God moved (Numbers 9:16–23). Are you ready for that? I am sure that sometimes they didn't feel like moving when God urged them to, but if they wanted to make it through the wilderness, they had to trust God's guidance.

We need to live in a state of readiness, like soldiers who have been put on alert. When that happens, soldiers know that they could be called to active duty at any moment. When doctors are on call, they must be ready at any moment to go and tend to a sick person. It doesn't matter what their plans are or what they are doing. When the call comes, they go.

At one of my conferences, I was looking through my Bible during worship, and all of a sudden it just came in my heart that I should give my Bible to a particular woman who had shared her testimony a few minutes earlier. I felt strongly that I should give it to her when I was done preaching that night. Now, I have to tell you: I wasn't expecting that at all, and I really liked that Bible; I had lots of notes in it. In fact, that Bible had notes on the seven greatest lessons I had learned in life written in it. But I strongly sensed the Lord was instructing me to give it to her. Now, I didn't know why God was asking me to move in that direction. Maybe it was really going to encourage that woman, or maybe the Lord was just seeing if I would be obedient. But whatever the reason, I had a choice to make: move in obedience or be disobedient. I did make the right decision that time, but there have been other times when I didn't, and I have always ended up regretting it.

The only way we can live without regret is to do the right thing now!

What is it that God has laid upon your heart to do? Has He asked you to forgive someone who hurt you? Bless someone who is struggling? Change a destructive habit? Let go of a dysfunctional relationship? Encourage a friend? Confront an issue? Whatever it is the Lord is asking you to do, don't hesitate another moment. Move in obedience and watch how God will bless each step you take. I truly believe that hopelessness comes with inactivity, but our hope flourishes when we are moving in step with God.

I recently heard that physically speaking, the more you move, the more you are able to move, and the less you move, the less you are able to move. If people retire and sit around and do nothing, their health often begins to fail, and they are able to do less and less. However, age doesn't seem to matter with those individuals who remain active and refuse to give up on life. Likewise, I believe that the more we promptly move with God, the easier it is to do. If you have been frozen in fear for a long time, it may take some extra effort to get going again, but it will be worth it.

If you feel that you need to move in some direction, but you're not sure what God is asking you to do and you feel stuck, let me ask you these two questions: (1) What was the last thing you felt God was telling you to do? (2) Did you do it? Sometimes God is waiting for us to obey His last instruction before He gives us a new one. With God, you can't skip steps—it's always one step at a time.

> Sometimes God is waiting for us to obey His last instruction before He gives us a new one.

Maybe the Lord put it on your heart to...

- Go back to school.
- Change the way you talk to your spouse.
- Have a joyful attitude.
- Take better care of yourself.
- Spend more time studying the Word.
- Start a Bible study.
- Give a gift to someone in need.
- Encourage your children more.
- Volunteer in your community.
- Serve in your church.
- Share your testimony with a friend.

We cannot skip steps just because we don't like the current one God is asking us to take. What would happen to a cake if we put in all the ingredients except the milk? We only left out one step, but it would be enough to ruin the entire cake. All of our other efforts and ingredients would be wasted simply because we decided to skip a step in the cake-baking process.

For many years God was asking me to have a more submissive attitude toward my husband, but I wasn't ready to take that step. I kept telling myself that I just couldn't do it, because I had been abused by men who tried to control me in my past. But, truthfully, it was just an excuse for disobedience. I was stuck and nothing was happening in my life or ministry because I was leaving out a step. When I finally took the step and followed the cloud of God's presence, good things started happening again.

Right Turn, Left Turn

In 1987, *The Los Angeles Times* published a story about a 53-year-old downhill snow-skier named Ed Kenan. Kenan was a businessman who loved to ski and was training to compete in the giant slalom event during the upcoming Winter Olympics. But there was something unusual about Ed Kenan: He was blind.

Seven years earlier, Kenan lost his vision, one eye at a time. Two operations couldn't stop detached retinas related to a diabetic condition from taking his eyesight. Dealing with an unspeakable hardship, Kenan had a choice to make: He could sit in darkness, feeling sorry for himself, mad that life had dealt him a bad hand, or he could keep moving. Kenan made his decision—six months after going blind, he was snow skiing down a slope in Vail, Colorado. "I forced myself to recover," he said. "I figured if I could ski down a mountain, I could do everything I put my mind to."

In 1983, Kenan won a gold medal in the giant slalom at the U.S. Association of Blind Athletes Alpine Competition held in Alta, Utah. Over the next few years, he would add to that medal count, winning several gold and silver medals in various competitions.

Not even blindness could keep Ed Kenan from living his life to the fullest.

When asked how it was possible to ski down mountain slopes and maneuver the various gates in the giant slalom, Ed explained that he had a sighted guide who would ski just ahead of him down the mountain. In a booming voice, his guide would shout "Go, go, go" when more speed was needed, and he would call out an exaggerated "Riiight turn," "Leeeft turn" as they approached the gates. All Kenan had to do was keep moving and trust the direction of his instructor. If he did, he would navigate the course flawlessly and cross the finish line safely.[1]

While the hardship you're dealing with may be different from Ed Kenan's, maybe you can relate in some small way. Maybe you know what it's like to suffer an unexpected loss. Maybe you understand how it feels to deal with a crushing disappointment. Maybe you're facing a frightening diagnosis. Maybe someone or something you thought would always be there is suddenly gone. And maybe you're asking yourself the question *Do I give up now, or do I find a way to keep going?*

Whatever darkness you're dealing with, let me remind you that you're not alone. God sees what you're going through, and He is right there with you. Isaiah 30:21 says, "And your ears will hear a word behind you, saying, This is the way; walk in it, when you turn to the right hand and when you turn to the left." That means God has promised to be your guide. When you can't see where to go, don't be afraid. Don't play possum!

Sometimes moving just means getting out of bed and cleaning your house, or going to work; other times it means following some specific direction from God. Either way, simple or more challenging, God wants us to be active so we don't atrophy spiritually! God will guide you and you'll hear Him say "Riiight turn," "Leeeft turn." The more you use your faith, the more faith you will have! Jesus said, "For to everyone who has will more be given, and he will be furnished richly so that he will have an abundance; but from the one who does not have, even what he does have will be taken away" (Matthew 25:29). He was speaking about the faith that was needed to take action instead of hiding in fear. Keep moving—it is one of the most powerful things you can do!

Get Your Hopes Up!

If you've found yourself stuck in life because of pain, an uncertainty, or a disappointment, I want to encourage you to get up and get moving. It may not be easy, but you can do it. Press through the things that would keep you stuck. Decide to do something rather than nothing. Be obedient to what the Lord is asking you to do.

God wants to deliver you from the quicksand of discouragement and hopelessness! So go ahead and get your hopes up. Even if you can't see it right now, God has a wonderful plan for your life. You're not going to hurt forever; you have a bright future ahead of you. Don't play possum another moment.

> *Therefore He says, Awake, O sleeper, and arise from the dead, and Christ shall shine (make day dawn) upon you and give you light.*
>
> Ephesians 5:14

SECTION III

HOPE AND HAPPINESS

. . . .

Happy (blessed, fortunate, enviable) is he who has the God of [special revelation to] Jacob for his help, whose hope is the Lord his God.

Psalm 146:5

I pray that you are beginning to see the power of hope and that you are realizing that your hope and happiness are closely linked. You cannot have faith without hope because hope is a positive expectation that something good is going to happen. I tried to exercise what I thought was faith for many years, but I had a negative attitude about life, and that certainly is not hope.

I was also unhappy much of the time, even though I was a Christian, had a lovely family, and was in full-time ministry. I didn't understand what was wrong and made the mistake most of us make, which is to think that if "things" would just change, then we could be happy. I was trying to use my faith to get God to change *things*, but I failed to realize that He wanted to change *me* much more than He wanted to change my circumstances.

He wanted me to learn to be happy in any situation, and that is possible only if we make a decision to be hopeful—to live with the happy anticipation that something good is about to happen to us, through us, and all around us.

As I mentioned, I am referring to this book as "The Happy Book"! I truly believe that if the principles in these pages are applied to your life, they will release any bottled-up joy you have been unable to uncork until now.

Keep saying "Something good is going to happen to me today" and "Something good is going to happen through me today."

CHAPTER 10

Look for the Good in Everything

"For I know the plans I have for you," declares the Lord, "plans to prosper you and not to harm you, plans to give you hope and a future."

Jeremiah 29:11 (NIV)

"I don't think of all the misery, but of the beauty that still remains."

—Anne Frank

There is a story of three men who found themselves working on a rather exceptional job site. These men were simple laborers who had been hired to help build a magnificent London cathedral already under construction. This cathedral had been designed by the renowned architect Sir Christopher Wren and was anticipated to be an architectural masterpiece. Writing about the rising cathedral, a London journalist asked the three men this simple question: "What are you doing here?" The first man answered, "I'm cutting stone for 10 shillings a day." The second man replied, "I'm putting in 10 hours a day on this job." But the third man gave a different answer altogether: "I'm helping Sir Christopher Wren construct one of London's greatest cathedrals."[1]

Isn't it amazing how your attitude can affect your outlook on life? What you choose to believe matters. The first worker believed money was the primary thing. When asked about his job, how much (or how little) he was making was the first thing he talked about. The second worker believed his time was of the utmost importance. When he was asked to describe what he was doing, he naturally talked about the many hours he spent working on the job. But the third worker chose to look past the money earned and the time involved. He didn't see this project as just another job. He saw it as a wonderful opportunity—a chance to build a great cathedral. He saw the best in his situation, and that caused him to be excited and joyful about the task at hand.

I believe one of the most valuable things you can do in order to live a hope-filled, joyful, overcoming life is to believe the best in every situation. That's not always easy to do. It's natural to find fault and assign blame—our flesh does that automatically. But seeing and believing the best is a choice. It's a decision you make to change the default setting in your life from negative to positive. Instead of assuming the worst, believe the best. Believe the best

> Instead of assuming the worst, believe the best.

about your co-worker. Believe the best about your church. Believe the best about your spouse. Believe the best about your health. Believe the best about your children. Believe the best about your future. You'd be amazed at how your entire outlook on life will change by simply believing the best about the people and the situations in your life.

Jesus gave us a new commandment, and that is to love one another as He has loved us. God's Word teaches us that love always believes the best (1 Corinthians 13:7). Actually, the Scripture says that love is "ever ready to believe the best" of everyone. Set your mind each morning to believe the best all throughout the day. I think it is something that we must do on purpose!

You can be like the first two laborers who showed up to work each morning seeing only a small paycheck and a long day ahead. They had uninspired attitudes and a dull outlook on life. Or you can be like the third worker who saw an opportunity instead of an obligation. He believed what he was doing was important, and he was excited about his assignment each day. It's simply a matter of perspective. All three had the same job, but only one actually enjoyed it.

Anytime I start finding it difficult to stay positive about what I am doing, it helps me tremendously to remember that I am serving Christ.

> *Whatever may be your task, work at it heartily (from the soul), as [something done] for the Lord and not for men.*
>
> *Knowing [with all certainty] that it is from the Lord [and not from men] that you will receive the inheritance which is your [real] reward. [The One Whom] you are actually serving [is] the Lord Christ (the Messiah).*
>
> Colossians 3:23–24

An Attitude of Hope

Hope and cynicism can't coexist. This is why it is so important to believe the best about the people in your life and the tasks you face from day to day—when you do, hope thrives and cynicism dies. If you'll say good-bye to a critical spirit and a complaining attitude, you'll discover an exciting new level of joy. You'll begin to appreciate the people you once took for granted, and you'll begin to see daily tasks as opportunities rather than obligations. It's amazing how a simple adjustment in perspective—choosing a godly perspective—can change your life.

Most people who are unhappy in life are unhappy because they focus on unhappy things. They see the worst in others, they talk about everything that's wrong in life, and they generally have a negative disposition. But hope does the opposite—hope sees the best, not the worst. That's why hope brings happiness. When you're expecting God to

> Hope sees the best, not the worst.

do something good, you can't help but be happy. Many people who are discouraged and frustrated in life feel that way simply because they're not expecting anything good to happen.

A lot of tragically painful and abusive things happened to me in the early years of my life, and because of that, I never really knew what it was like to be happy. At the age of 23, I married Dave, and after a few weeks, I remember him asking "What is wrong with you? Why are you so negative about everything?" I told him, "Well, if you don't expect anything good to happen, you won't be disappointed when it doesn't." Can you imagine anybody saying that? Well, I said it, and I meant it at that time in my life.

Those words had become my philosophy in life. I thought I was protecting myself from being hurt and disappointed by not expecting anything good to happen. I could spot the negative in almost any situation because that was what I was used to experiencing. Thankfully, over the years, God has taught me a lot about hope. He's changed my attitude and shown me the importance of setting my mind and keeping it set on Him and His Word. I'm no longer a person who expects bad things to happen. I do what I am urging you to do. I purposely look for and expect good things. I also take time regularly to recount anything good that I notice God has done for me or through me. The more you become aware of God's goodness, the more you will live each day with excitement and expectation.

Hope has everything to do with attitude. And I think that with God's help, you and I can have a positive attitude about everything that happens in life...no matter what the situation is. If you want to be a person full of hope and happiness, no matter what happens during the course of your day, choose to trust God and have a positive outlook by believing the best in any situation.

- If your child wakes up with a cold and can't go to school, choose to have a positive outlook. Thank God that it's just a cold and nothing worse.

- If the sink springs a leak, leaving water all over the kitchen floor, thank God that you were home when it happened and caught it before it made an even bigger mess.
- If the dry cleaner ruins one of your outfits, choose to have a positive outlook. Now you've got an excuse to go shopping.
- If you lose your job, choose to be positive. Now you have the opportunity to get a better one.

Whatever unexpected challenge or frustration you may face, decide in advance that you're not going to let it steal your joy. Being unhappy does nothing except make you miserable, so don't waste your time with it. Don't let the daily events of life determine what kind of life you're going to live. Choose to smile even in the midst of irritating circumstances, and refuse to let something as silly as a traffic jam or a bad hair day keep you from enjoying your life.

> *Whatever unexpected challenge or frustration you may face, decide in advance that you're not going to let it steal your joy.*

Beauty for Ashes

Seeing the best in any situation and keeping a positive outlook is possible only because of the promises found in God's Word. In Romans 8:28 (NIV), the apostle Paul says: "And we know that in all things God works for the good of those who love him, who have been called according to his purpose." Notice that the verse doesn't say God works *some* things together for your good; it says *all* things. Every situation, every encounter, every trial, every frustration— God is going to work it *all* out for your good.

God can even take the most difficult things you've been through and use them for your good. Isaiah 61:3 (NKJV) says that He will give you "beauty for ashes" and "the oil of joy for mourning." God didn't cause the pain or the dysfunction you've suffered, but He can heal your wounds and use what you've been through to accomplish something beautiful—for your life and for others.

I have personally found that believing God will work something good out of any current dilemma I am experiencing really helps me get through it with a hopeful attitude. It is a wonderful promise that I have seen work time after time just the way God promises. It worked for me when I had breast cancer, in overcoming sexual abuse in my childhood, when friends I trusted turned against me, and in countless other situations. Whatever you may be going through right now, believe and say "God will work this out for my good," and you will feel a lift in your mood.

Enjoy the Wait

If I were to ask you "What is one of the most difficult times to be happy and hopeful?"—there's a good chance you would tell me it's when you're waiting on God to answer a prayer or meet a need. It could even be when you're waiting in traffic, or waiting for your spouse to get ready to go somewhere with you and you are late. It may be when you are waiting in a line at the grocery store and the clerk is new and taking a long time to check out your groceries. It might be waiting for changes in people you have prayed for, or even breakthroughs in habits you have struggled with. It's never easy to wait, but it's something we all have to do at times in our lives. I've known a lot of people who lose all peace and joy while they're waiting. One of the people I know very well, because the person is me! Thankfully, I have made progress over the years, but I am still growing in "waiting well."

> We can experience the joy of the Lord even in the times when we're waiting.

I believe we can experience the joy of the Lord even in the times when we're waiting. It all depends on how we choose to wait. Isaiah 40:31 says: "But those who wait for the Lord [who expect, look for, and hope in Him] shall change and renew their strength...." You can be strengthened in the waiting process, but only if you wait with hope—expecting, looking, and hoping in Him. There's no benefit from being frustrated, impatient, and miserable while you're waiting on God. But if you'll have an attitude of expectation and anticipation, the season of waiting can actually be a great time in your life. Even when we are waiting in a line at the grocery store, we can choose to believe the best by believing that our time is in His hands, as He says in Scripture. Perhaps God is saving us from some accident by delaying our departure, or He may be using the discipline of "divine delay" to help us mature spiritually.

You may be praying and waiting for financial provision, a physical or emotional healing, a spouse, a career opportunity, or a child to return home. Whatever it is, you can have joy in the waiting if you'll believe the best...even before you receive it. Kind of like this boy:

> A man approached a Little League baseball game one afternoon. He asked a boy in the dugout what the score was. The boy responded, "18 to nothing—we're behind."
>
> "Boy," said the spectator, "I'll bet you're discouraged."
>
> "Why should I be discouraged?" replied the boy. "We haven't even gotten up to bat yet!"[2]

I love this simple story and the hope of this young boy. The assumption is that this Little Leaguer should be upset and discouraged. His team is getting creamed, and it's still the first inning. Things aren't looking very good as he and his teammates wait for their turn to bat.

But rather than getting negative and depressed about what things look like in the waiting process, this young baseball player chose to have a different attitude. He believed the best, assuming that his team was going to score more than 18 runs when his period of waiting was over. Instead of getting discouraged while he waited, he got excited.

If you're waiting on something today, don't let the external appearances steal your hope and crush your joy. It might not look like the relationship can be restored, it might not look like the finances will come in, it might not look like the condition will change, it might not look like things are going to work out—but instead of getting discouraged while you're waiting, get excited. You haven't had your turn to bat yet. Believe the best. Trust that God is going to supply exactly what you need at the very moment you need it.

> Instead of getting discouraged while you're waiting, get excited.

If you'll determine to believe the best, even before you see the results, times of waiting can be exciting seasons of hopeful anticipation.

"How to" Believe the Best

1 Corinthians 13:7 says that "love…is ever ready to believe the best of every person, its hopes are fadeless under all circumstances, and it endures everything [without weakening]." What a wonderful Scripture—love always believes the best about people and never gives up hope. Wouldn't that be a great way to live? *Ever ready to believe the best of every person* and *having a hope that is fadeless under all circumstances*? Well, that's the kind of joy-filled, hopeful life God wants you to live.

> Today can be the day you say good-bye to a cynical attitude and hello to hope.

If you've failed to believe the best about one or more of the people in your life, it's hurting you more than it's hurting them. Today can be the day you say good-bye to a cynical attitude and hello to hope. Here are a few practical ways you can do that.

Take a Closer Look

- Ask God to show you something good about that person, and then take the time to look closer than ever before. You already know what you don't like; discover something you do like.
- Instead of "finding faults," try "finding favorites." Find a favorite thing about that person—something you may have overlooked in the past. Instead of looking at their problems, see their potential.

Assume Something Good

- Many times we assume the worst about a person. *That person is going to disappoint me, they hurt me on purpose, I know they will eventually leave me.* But instead of assuming the worst, hope always assumes the best. That person may have messed up in the past, but it's possible she's learned from her mistakes. Assume she is going to bless and impress you and then give her the chance to do so.

See People the Way God Sees Them

- There is a big difference between the way God sees people and the way we see people. For example, when the crowds came to Jesus, the disciples saw them as a chore, but Jesus saw them with compassion. Ask the Lord to open your eyes to see His people the way He sees them—with eyes of love, understanding, and compassion.

Have an "I Hope" Mentality Rather Than an "I Hate" Mentality

- This takes some practice, but it's a fun exercise. Start hoping for the good things in a person rather than hating the annoying things about him. Verbalize hope language. Try saying things like: "I hope this works out," "I hope you're right," and "I'm hopeful about this relationship," instead of "I hate making new friends," "I hate dealing with that person," or "I hate when they say that."

These are some good steps to get you started, but it's not an all-inclusive list. If you really want to know how to be full of hope, believing the best about others and about the circumstances of your life, study the example of Jesus. Read the Gospels and watch how Jesus ministered, healed, encouraged, taught, and loved. Jesus didn't just want the best for people; He saw the best in them too. What a great example to follow. Aren't you glad that Jesus saw the best in you? He saw something worth saving! You and I can make a decision to do that same thing for other people. Let's begin today!

> Jesus didn't just want the best for people; He saw the best in them too.

Get Your Hopes Up!

There is a joy that comes with looking and believing for the best. It's like being a gold miner who believes he's about to strike it rich. When you approach the people and the circumstances in your life with a hopeful attitude, you're bound to find something good.

Don't let the frustrations of the day steal your joy. Be positive enough to smile right through daily inconveniences. And if you're dealing with something bigger than an inconvenience, remember that God promises to work all things out for good. So go ahead and get your hopes up. Good things are going to happen today...and tomorrow...and the day after that. All you have to do is look for them.

CHAPTER 11

Prisoners of Hope

Return to the stronghold [of security and prosperity], you
prisoners of hope; even today do I declare that I will restore
double your former prosperity to you.

Zechariah 9:12

"Hope is the dream of a waking man."

—Aristotle

A story is told involving a school system in a large city that had a special program designed to help students keep up with their assignments during lengthy stays in the city's hospitals. One day a teacher who was working in the program received a routine call, asking her to take a homework assignment to a particular child. She briefly spoke with the child's teacher and took down the boy's name and room number. "We're studying nouns and adverbs in his class now," the regular teacher explained. "I'd be grateful if you could help him understand these concepts so he doesn't fall too far behind."

The teacher assigned to the hospital program went to see the boy later that evening. However, when giving the assignment, no one thought to mention to her how badly the boy was burned or the amount of pain he was dealing with. Upset at the sight of the hurting student, the teacher awkwardly stammered, "I've been sent by your school to help you with nouns and adverbs." When she left the hospital that night, she felt like she had accomplished very little.

But the next day, when she returned to the hospital, a nurse ran up to her and asked, "What did you do to that boy?" Feeling she must have done something wrong, the teacher began to apologize. "No, no," said the enthusiastic nurse. "You don't know what I mean. We've been worried about that little boy, but ever since yesterday, his whole attitude has changed. He's fighting back and responding to treatment. It's as though he's decided to live."

Two weeks later, the boy explained what happened. Before the teacher assigned to the hospital arrived, he had completely given up hope. But everything changed when she showed up in his hospital room. He came to a simple realization, and he explained it this way, "They wouldn't send a teacher to work on nouns and adverbs with a dying boy, would they?"[1]

The power of hope is amazing. Stuck in a hospital room, surrounded by sickness, discouragement, and bad news, the boy was ready to give up. But just one teacher with a helpful demeanor and a homework assignment brought enough hope to turn the boy's outlook on life around and give him a reason to keep going. If one person could bring that much hope, imagine what would happen if you surrounded yourself with people like that on a regular basis. What could five people, or 10 people, or 20 people like that do?

Think of what that might look like in your life. The truth is: You are going to be influenced and deeply affected by what is around you. If you fill your life with people, events, and activities that foster hope, then you're going to be filled with hope and optimism. But if you fill your life with hopeless people and choose to partake in activities that are discouraging and negative, you're going to be frustrated and miserable on a regular basis. It's all a matter of what you choose to surround yourself with every day.

This doesn't mean that we can avoid all negativity in life. Some of what we find ourselves surrounded with is not necessarily by choice, but we can make the best choices possible.

The Hope That Surrounds You

Zechariah 9:12 uses an interesting phrase when it refers to our relationship with hope. In this verse of Scripture, God refers to His people as "prisoners of hope." He says, "Return to the stronghold [of security and prosperity], you *prisoners of hope*..." (emphasis added).

I like this description—"prisoners of hope." Think about it. If you're a prisoner of hope, you have no choice about it: You can't be negative, you can't be a worrier, you can't be hopeless. When times are tough, and when you're dealing with disappointment, the hope that surrounds you will cause you to rise up in faith. Everything around you is telling you God can make a way, and when that happens, something stirs in your spirit. You are emboldened to believe and declare, "Good things are happening to me and through me!"

My first title choice for this book was "Prisoners of Hope," but we were concerned that people might not understand it without explanation, so we decided on *Get Your Hopes Up!* I love the thought of being so hopeful that it is like being imprisoned in it. Are you ready to live your life locked in a prison of hope?

God wants us to be locked up in hope, trusting that He can change what needs to be changed. Our hope is in God! He can do anything! No matter what we feel like or how things look, we believe that God is working and that we will see positive change at just the right time. That's why hope is determined and doesn't give up. When you come to the end of your rope—when your strength falters and fails—the story isn't over. There is no limit to God's strength. His strength is inexhaustible. If you will be steadfast in your hope, you can't lose...because God can't lose. Since God is for you, the victory is sure.

God called me into the ministry many years ago, but I have to be honest with you and say that success didn't happen overnight. There was a lot of hard work involved, and there were many nights when I wondered if I heard God correctly. People weren't always receptive to me, and there were a lot of meetings where I wondered if anyone would show up at all. Dave and I walked through years and years of preparation and trusting God to build up what is now a worldwide ministry. During those years, I was tempted to quit many times. But my testimony is: I'm still here! Even when I had questions and doubts, even when I didn't think I had the strength to go on, I knew that God could make a way when there seemed to be no way. Dave and I put our hope in Him, and He exceeded our wildest expectations.

If you make the decision to be a prisoner of hope—to live surrounded by the happy anticipation that God is going to do something good—the same thing can happen for you. Whatever goal or dream God has placed in your heart, you're going to see it come to pass. It might not happen when you thought it would happen, and it might not happen the way you thought it would happen, but God is going to work in such a way as to exceed your wildest expectations too. You won't have to make it happen in your strength. All you have to do is persevere—just don't give up. Surround yourself with hope and watch God bless you in ways you never thought possible.

> Surround yourself with hope and watch God bless you in ways you never thought possible.

...Eye has not seen and ear has not heard and has not entered into the heart of man, [all that] God has prepared (made and keeps ready) for those who love Him [who hold Him in affectionate reverence, promptly obeying Him and gratefully recognizing the benefits He has bestowed].

1 Corinthians 2:9

I believe that God has many pleasant surprises waiting for you, things He has prepared that are waiting for you. Keep your hopes up!

Things You Can't Take with You

When a prisoner walks into his cell, he can't bring any contraband with him. No outside or unapproved items are allowed in his environment. Those things are considered dangerous and are therefore not allowed.

Well, you're a different kind of prisoner—you're a prisoner of hope. You're not surrounded by bricks and iron; God wants to surround you with His goodness, with His grace, with His hope. No matter where you turn, no matter where you look, you can experience joy, peace, confidence, and the blessings of God. This is the life Jesus died to give you.

But it's important to understand that there are some things you can't bring with you when you enter the environment of hope because they're dangerous. If you're going to be surrounded by hope, here's a list of contraband you have the opportunity to leave behind:

- Negative words
- A victim mentality
- Comparing yourself to others
- A sour outlook on life
- Murmuring and complaining
- An attitude of self-pity
- Discouragement and despair

The life of the believer isn't meant to be oppressed by these burdens of the enemy. You don't have to live depressed and without hope. With God's help, you can get rid of every discouraging, self-centered,

> You can build your life on the truth of God's Word rather than the lies of the enemy.

negative lie from the enemy and live in an environment of hope. You can build your life on the truth of God's Word rather than the lies of the enemy.

A Scripture I quote often is 1 Peter 5:7. It says:

Cast the whole of your care [all your anxieties, all your worries, all your concerns, once and for all] on Him, for He cares for you affectionately and cares about you watchfully.

We are to "cast" our care. That word means to pitch or throw! Isn't that a great picture? We don't just take off our cares and set them in a chair beside us where we can pick them up again later; we cast them completely away. We throw them as far as we can, never to be picked up again. We cast them on God and He takes care of us!

Reject the lies that say *Nobody likes me. Nobody's going to want to eat lunch with me. I'll never shake this illness. I won't get the promotion at work. I'll probably never get married.* Don't surround yourself with those hopeless thoughts. Cast each care on God the moment you sense its presence, and things in your life will begin to blossom. The anxiety and the worry that used to weigh you down suddenly have no power over you anymore. Now you can experience what Jesus calls "relief and ease and refreshment and recreation and blessed quiet" for your soul (see Matthew 11:29).

The Garden of Hope

I have mentioned that if we live in the garden of hope, something is always blooming. There are usually lots of different kinds of flowers planted in a garden, and something is teeming with new life all the time. Just about the time one type is finished blossoming, another type begins to blossom. The owners of this garden are never without flowers in their lives. We have three varieties of bushes at our home with different flowers on them. One blooms in early spring, another in late spring, and another in early summer. We have flowers all the time!

I have realized that I won't enjoy the flowers, no matter how many there are, if I don't take time to look at them. Likewise, we need to take time to look at the good things that are happening around us on a regular basis. The media reports everything bad that is happening in the world, but there are good things all around us if we purposely look for them.

At times we get so busy dealing with our problems that we don't take time to search for the good in life. I think it is important for us to do what each crisis demands during times of adversity and to take time to see the good in life. We might say that the good is the counterbalance for the difficulty. It is like adding salt or spices to bland food. Somehow, we find greater strength to deal with our challenges in life when we take time to see what is blooming each day in our garden of hope.

I decided to take a few minutes away from writing and see what is blooming in my garden today. I found that I feel really good, I remembered that I slept great last night, the sun is shining, I have already talked to three of my four children and it is only 10:30 a.m., and my husband hugged me this morning. However, one of my grandchildren is going through a difficult time, a good friend has cancer, I have a lot of work to do this week, and my phone is broken. Nothing that comes under the category of "problem" is more than we can handle joyfully if we always take time to look at what is blooming in our garden of hope.

Maybe you have not noticed it, but I feel certain something is blooming in your life. I encourage you to take time to look for it.

Improve Your Environment

Sometimes we have to fight for hope. We must push past the voices in the world that try to drown it out. It is important to surround ourselves with people who are not negative and gloomy. At the very least, we need some people in our lives who are hopeful and who spread hope. It is easy when we are hurting or dealing with painful issues to gravitate toward people we can rehearse our troubles to. There is nothing wrong with sharing our pain with a friend, or asking for prayer, but we should not pick people who are already hopeless themselves. You may tell a negative friend about the pit you're in, and she will say, "You haven't seen a real pit until you see my pit." You know the type I am talking about.

I want to encourage you to improve your surroundings today. Tune out the negative voices and surround yourself with hope instead. Ask God to bring people into your life who will encourage you on a daily basis. Instead of hanging around people who will remind you of your problems, find some people who will tell you that you can make it and that God is on your side. It is easy to excuse our hopelessness by saying "I am around so many negative people who drag me down. My job is depressing, and everyone complains all day." This is when you have to fight for hope. Take the responsibility for finding some people who are not negative, and don't listen to the office gossip. Instead of eating at the lunch table with complainers, go out and take a walk. If you have a negative influence in your home and it is one you cannot avoid, at least counterbalance the negative influence with other positive relationships that will give you a break from hopeless people occasionally.

> Tune out the negative voices and surround yourself with hope instead.

Make studying God's Word a priority in your life. The Word has power in it to lift up our heads and give us hope in any situation.

Another thing you can do to surround yourself with hope is to listen to worship music and good Bible teaching. With the technology available today, there are more opportunities than ever to watch and listen to life-giving messages and encouraging music. Whether it's a CD, a podcast, an app on your phone, a streaming video—whatever is convenient for you and your schedule—make time to surround yourself with the Word of God on a daily basis.

The enemy may surround us with people who are plotting wickedness and circumstances that are painful, but God's Word teaches us that He surrounds us with His presence and many good things.

> *You are my hiding place; you will protect me from trouble and surround me with songs of deliverance.*
>
> Psalm 32:7 (NIV)

> *As the mountains surround Jerusalem, so the Lord surrounds his people both now and forevermore.*
>
> Psalm 125:2 (NIV)

Get Your Hopes Up!

If you've been surrounded by negativity, doubt, uncertainty, worry, or disappointment in your life, it is time for a change. You don't have to let those things rule your life any longer. You can change your environment—you can live in hope. Even before you have a change in your situation, you can have a change in your soul. You can choose to be a prisoner of hope and look forward to God restoring a double portion of anything you have lost in life.

CHAPTER 12

Be an Answer to Someone's Prayer

*Let each of you esteem and look upon and be concerned for
not [merely] his own interests, but also each for the interests
of others.*

Philippians 2:4

"There are no hopeless situations; there are only people
who have grown hopeless about them."

—Clare Boothe Luce

If you want to truly experience hope and happiness in your life,
the best thing you can do is help someone else. I know that sounds
counterintuitive, but it works. Taking the focus off yourself and
looking for ways to bless others takes your mind off your own problems, and as you give hope and encouragement to them through
words or acts of service, you receive a harvest of everything you
give multiplied many times over.

When a farmer plants a garden, he puts tiny seeds in the ground,
and after a while he gets back an entire garden of plants that provide
food for him and his family. God's promise that we will reap what
we sow still amazes me. If we want something, all we need to do is
start giving some of it away!

Gary Morsch, founder of Heart to Heart International in Kansas
City, is a physician who has done much work to provide medical
equipment and supplies for the poor in countries all over the world.

In his book *The Power of Serving Others*, he tells a story of volunteering at Mother Teresa's Home for the Dying Destitutes in Calcutta, India.

The Home for the Dying Destitutes is a ministry center where the infirm were brought when it was clear they were going to die. If they had no one to care for them and no money to pay for aid, they were brought to this home, where Mother Teresa and her volunteers would help them. Some of the worst illnesses imaginable were seen here, and the poorest of the poor were cared for every day.

Knowing the desperate need and armed with confidence and medical expertise, Morsch was enthusiastic upon arrival. Optimistically, he thought, *I'm going to put this place out of business. Because of my help, they're going to have to change the name.* His heart was in the right place and his intentions were good, but he wasn't ready for what happened next.

When he and his team of 90 volunteers showed up to serve, Sister Priscilla, a soft-spoken nun with a gentle British accent, started assigning tasks. Morsch carefully placed his stethoscope around his neck in a not-so-subtle attempt to let Sister Priscilla know he was a doctor. Surely she would give him an important task suited to his professional abilities and credentials.

After sending everyone else off to serve in a variety of jobs, Sister Priscilla looked at the last volunteer standing in front of her, Gary Morsch. "Follow me, please," she directed. They entered the men's ward, filled with cots of sick and dying men. *Well, I guess this will be my assignment,* Morsch thought, but Sister Priscilla walked right through the ward and on to the next. Entering the women's ward— full of emaciated women in the final stages of life—Morsch assumed, *The need must be greatest here. This is where they'll put me to work,* but Sister Priscilla kept walking. When they entered the kitchen where rice was being prepared over an open fire, he began to get worried. *Why would they want a doctor to serve in the kitchen?* he wondered, but Sister Priscilla proceeded quickly through the kitchen too.

Exiting the kitchen and leading Morsch into a narrow outdoor alley, Sister Priscilla pointed to an extremely large pile of rotting garbage. The smell was enough to make Morsch want to gag. "We need you to take this garbage down the street to the dump," she explained. "The dump is several blocks down and on the right. You can't miss it." With that, she gave the doctor two buckets, a shovel, and a parting smile, and left him to his work.

Morsch stood there confused and a little offended. He wondered what he should do. Should he refuse the task? Should he talk to someone about a new assignment? After a minute or two of consideration, he decided to do the only thing he could do—get to work. All day long, the esteemed doctor carried buckets full of putrid garbage to the city dump. At the end of the day, he was a sweaty, smelly mess, but he moved the entire disgusting pile.

Upset and angry about the events of the day, Morsch headed back through the kitchen, the women's ward, and then the men's ward looking to collect his team and go back to where they were staying. As he walked back through these rooms, he couldn't help but feel that his services should have been put to better use. Even helping in the kitchen would have been better than hauling garbage. And that's when he saw it. Waiting to say a halfhearted good-bye to Sister Priscilla, Morsch noticed a small, hand-lettered sign that read, in Mother Teresa's own words, "We can do no great things, only small things with great love."

That moment was a turning point for Gary Morsch. He said, "My heart melted. I completely missed the point. I needed this lesson. Serving others is not about how much I know, how many degrees I've earned, or what my credentials are. It is about attitude and availability to do whatever is needed—with love."

Gary Morsch went on to become a dear friend to Mother Teresa, and he found a special purpose in life in helping other people. He brought many more groups back to Calcutta to minister to the poorest of the poor in India, and each time he took great satisfaction in seeing his team of volunteers impacted by the experience. He explained, "Often the volunteers come with the same kind of certainty, full of themselves, as I was. But every one of them is transformed in the act of serving others."[1]

Give Hope to Get Hope

Acts 20:35 says:

> ...*We ought to assist the weak, being mindful of the words of the Lord Jesus, how He Himself said, It is more blessed (makes one happier and more to be envied) to give than to receive.*

Jesus said that happiness comes when you help others. This is the opposite of what we assume to be true. We think that if we focus on ourselves, working diligently to pursue happiness, then we'll eventually find it. If we earn more money, collect enough possessions, accomplish enough goals, lose a certain number of pounds, gain a measure of recognition—then, and only then, will we be happy. This causes us to work harder and harder so that one day we might achieve happiness.

I can tell you, there are a lot of tired people out there. The pursuit of happiness can be an exhausting venture. I know, because I lived it for a long time. For many years of my life, I was a miserable Christian. I loved God, but I was rarely happy. It didn't take much to upset me and ruin my day. If the car started making a funny noise, if Dave went golfing instead of spending a Saturday morning with me, if one of my kids argued with me, if I didn't accomplish all the things on my to-do list—if any one of these things happened, I gave up all hope of having a good day. And the harder I worked, trying to achieve happiness, the more elusive happiness seemed.

But God showed me a lot during those days about how to enjoy my life. The more I studied the Word, the more I saw that the thoughts I was thinking, the words I was speaking, and the attitudes I was embracing had a significant impact on the life I was living. I learned that I didn't have to be controlled by my feelings and my emotions. With God's help, I could live beyond them and enjoy the life Christ died to give me.

I've spent many years writing about and teaching principles from God's Word on each of those topics, but one of the simplest and most powerful things God showed me is this: If we want to have hope and happiness, we need to *give* hope and happiness. When you take your eyes off your problems and look to helping others with their problems, it's amazing what God will do.

Every time I would set my frustrations and needs aside and concentrate on helping someone around me, my whole attitude would change. Instead of praying "God, I need this…" or "Lord, why don't I have that?"—I started praying "God, how can I help someone today?" and "Lord, give me an opportunity to meet a need." I discovered there is an unspeakable joy in being used by God to answer someone else's prayer.

You've probably noticed the same thing in your life. It truly is more blessed to give than to receive. You're never going to earn enough, collect enough, or achieve enough to fill the happiness gap. Vanity is never satisfied. But the moment you stop looking inward and start looking outward, you'll discover a hope and happiness you never knew existed. Like Gary Morsch and his teams of volunteers, you'll be "transformed in the act of serving others."

> The moment you stop looking inward and start looking outward, you'll discover a hope and happiness you never knew existed.

I ask God daily to show me someone I can help. Sometimes what He leads me to do is something major, but many times it is something small. Sometimes it seems almost unnoticeable. Today a man came to fix my toilet, and when he was finished he asked if he could speak with me for a moment. Once I said yes, he went on to tell me he had a wife and five children and wanted to know which of my books might be good for him to give his wife for Mother's Day. I talked with him for a little while about his family and then I took him to my personal bookshelves and let him choose two of my books as a gift for his wife. It took only a few minutes and was not costly to me, but it meant a lot to him. Somehow, I believe I will be happier today because of that one tiny act of kindness. I regret that it took me so long to learn this amazing principle, but I am grateful to know it now. We can fight against hopelessness every day of our lives through random acts of kindness!

Even the Greatest Serve

During the American Revolution, a man in civilian clothes rode past a group of soldiers repairing a small defensive barrier. Their leader was shouting instructions but making no attempt to help them. When asked "why?" by the rider, the leader retorted with great dignity, "Sir, I am a corporal!"

The stranger apologized, dismounted, and proceeded to help the exhausted soldiers. The job done, he turned to the corporal and said, "Mr. Corporal, next time you have a job like this and not enough men to do it, go to your commander-in-chief, and I will come and help you again." The stranger was none other than George Washington.[2]

No matter how important you become, never allow yourself to believe you're too important to help someone else. You may have worked a long time, you may have achieved a lot in your personal and professional life,

> *No matter how important you become, never allow yourself to believe you're too important to help someone else.*

and you may have respected titles before your name or impressive initials after it, but you are never too important to humble yourself and help others. Jesus came down from a high and lofty place and humbled Himself to the lowest degree (Philippians 2:7). We are taught in Scripture to let Him be our example in humility (Philippians 2:5).

I have the privilege of being the president of a worldwide ministry. Over the course of any given day, there are a lot of decisions I have to make and a lot of places I need to be. I'm thankful for the opportunities God has given me, but some of the most joyful moments in my life aren't spent meeting in a boardroom or preaching on a stage. As much as I enjoy those things, some of the most joyful and satisfying moments in my life are when I get to serve people through our Hand of Hope outreaches. Every time I get to stand with our volunteers and spend a little bit of time blessing others—handing out food to the hungry, providing clean water wells for the thirsty, giving school supplies to the poor—it reminds me why we do what we do. In reaching out to others with a hand of hope, I receive fresh hope and happiness myself. Many times I have left the mission field in a third-world country exhausted, but I've never walked away from a trip regretting the opportunity I had to serve.

We began the missions arm of our ministry almost 20 years ago, and I felt that we should name it Hand of Hope because reaching out to hopeless people with hope was our goal. I think it might be safe to say that it would be impossible for individuals to feel hopeless themselves if they regularly give hope to others!

Jesus is the Son of God who came to take away the sins of the world, but even He took time to serve. In Mark 10:45, Jesus said that He "came not to have service rendered to Him, but to serve, and to give His life as a ransom for (instead of) many." Time after time in the Gospels, we see Jesus helping others: feeding the crowds, healing the sick, spending time with the children, and even wash-

ing the disciples' feet. Jesus must have
found tremendous joy in serving others, because He did it all the time. He
left us this example so that we might
follow in His footsteps.

> Jesus must have found tremendous joy in serving others, because He did it all the time.

What a great example to follow. Don't
get too important or too busy to give
hope to someone in need. Take time each day to look for a person
you can bless. It may be just a simple gesture of kindness, or it may
be a significant act of generosity—whatever you can do to help a person in need, I encourage you to do it. Not only is that person going to
be blessed by your act of service, you're going to be blessed too.

The Best Way to Tell People about Jesus Is to Show Them Jesus

Romans 2:4 (NKJV) teaches that it is the goodness of God that leads
men to repentance. You'd be surprised how many of your friends,
neighbors, and co-workers would want to accept Jesus if you'd just
be good to them. Sometimes we need to stop preaching to everybody and just start being kind to the people in our lives—take a
genuine interest in them and bless them, pray for them and ask God
to make us aware of how we might serve them. In other words, we
should "show" people the love of Jesus!

James 2:15–16 says:

> If a brother or sister is poorly clad and lacks food for each
> day, And one of you says to him, Good-bye! Keep [yourself]
> warm and well fed, without giving him the necessities for the
> body, what good does that do?

Let's not be people who say, "Good-bye! Keep yourself warm
and well fed." If someone has a need, and if you can meet the need,

then do it. Too often we dismiss a need by saying "I will pray for you," without even asking God to show us what we might do to help. I have learned that I don't need to

> If you're going to pray that God will help someone, be ready for Him to send you to do it.

pray and ask God to meet a need that I could easily meet myself but perhaps just don't want to do so. If you're going to pray that God will help someone, be ready for Him to send you to do it.

One person said he went as part of a group to Russia to hand out Bibles during a particularly hard time when a lot of people were starving. The team took their Bibles to a soup line where people were waiting to get a small piece of bread and a bowl of soup. As one man attempted to hand a Bible to a woman, she became angry and said, "Your Bible doesn't fill up my empty belly." It was as if she resented the Christians for telling them about a good God while offering no tangible, practical help. Those believers who were handing out Bibles never forgot that. I believe that some people are hurting so badly that they would not even be able to hear the Gospel if we didn't do something to relieve their pain first.

Now, of course I'm not saying we shouldn't give people Bibles, but I am saying that besides giving them the Word, we need to meet their needs. That's what Jesus did. Jesus gave people the Word *and* He met their needs. He fed them; He healed them; He taught them; and He listened to them. He did more than talk about the goodness of the Father; He *demonstrated* that goodness in real ways.

If there are people in your life today who need to know Jesus, let me suggest you try a new method of sharing the Gospel. Instead of just telling them about the hope found in Christ, give them that hope. Find out what needs they have and ask God to help you meet those needs. Maybe they need groceries, gasoline for their cars, or money to go to the doctor. Maybe they need a babysitter so they can have a night to relax. Maybe they just need someone to listen. Whatever you can do to show them the love of Jesus, do it. When you help people with their physical needs, you'll be surprised at how quickly they open up about their spiritual needs.

> *When you help people with their physical needs, you'll be surprised at how quickly they open up about their spiritual needs.*

Get Your Hopes Up!

It's important to remember that life isn't just about ourselves. We may be going through personal difficulty in our lives, and when we are, it's easy to get totally focused on asking God to help *us*, to meet *our* needs, to provide the things *we* feel *we're* missing. But in the midst of dealing with the issues that directly affect you, don't forget about the people around you. Everywhere you look, there are friends, relatives, co-workers, neighbors, and strangers who have a need—a need you may be able to meet.

The best way to receive hope is to give it away. In God's economy, the last are first (see Matthew 20:16), the least are the greatest (see Luke 9:48), the weak are strong (see Joel 3:10), and when you give you receive (see Luke 6:38). So go ahead and get your hopes up. You can discover a whole new way to enjoy your life simply by helping others enjoy theirs. Look around you and see whom you can help— I promise you won't have to look very hard. Someone you know is praying and asking God for help right now. Maybe you can be the answer to that prayer!

CHAPTER 13

Hope Is Our Anchor

We have this hope as an anchor of the soul, firm and secure....

Hebrews 6:19 (NIV)

"It's silly not to hope."
—Ernest Hemingway, *The Old Man and the Sea*

I believe God wants us to be stable and enjoy life no matter what is going on around us. He wants us to be solidly anchored in Him and to be hopeful at all times. I think one of the best testimonies we have as believers is our joy. We have so much to celebrate! We've been forgiven, healed, and set free. And not only did Jesus die to make a way for us to spend eternity in Heaven, but He promises that we can enjoy every day of our lives here on Earth. Christians should be the happiest people on the planet!

> Christians should be the happiest people on the planet!

Although we are God's children, we do have trials and tribulations, and often we let them dictate our thoughts, moods, and attitudes. We let them steal our smile, and that is tragic because I believe the joy of the Lord on our faces is a great advertisement for Jesus! How can any difficulty make us unhappy for very long when we have the promise that God works all things out for good for those who love Him and who are seeking His purpose for their life?

Joy and happiness aren't luxuries or mere options—they are essential aspects of our lives in Christ. Nehemiah 8:10 says: "...And be not grieved and depressed, for the joy of the Lord is your strength..." and Romans 14:17 (NIV) says the kingdom of God is a matter of "righteousness, peace and joy in the Holy Spirit." Joy is vitally important if you are going to live a victorious, overcoming life.

Hope: The Natural Cure for Unhappiness

Joy and hope go hand in hand. When you begin to really live in hope—believing and trusting that God is going to do amazing things in your life—joy comes rushing in. You couldn't be depressed or discouraged even if you wanted to. Hope is the natural cure for unhappiness.

> Hope is the natural cure for unhappiness.

Why not do an experiment to see if my belief in this area is correct and will work for you? The next time you are experiencing a sad, depressed day, take the time to think *God is working my problems out for my good and I am expecting something good to happen to me.* Now try saying the same thing out loud, and repeat this process throughout the day. It may not be how you feel, but it is the truth! God's truth has the power to overcome our feelings if we give it the opportunity to do so.

When we have hope in God's goodness, it stabilizes our frantic thoughts and emotions. It calms us down and cheers us up. Our soul (mind, will, and emotions) finds its place of peace in God's promise. If people have no hope, it is impossible for them to remain stable in the storms of life. They have nothing to anchor them to any foundation that is not shaky. If we have no hope in God, what exists in the world that we can trust as a permanent place of safety? The honest answer has to be "There is nothing!"

Instead of merely "trying" to feel better or thinking that you can't feel better until your circumstance changes, give God's Word a chance to work in your life.

Life can be so much fun. I made my mind up many years ago that I was going to enjoy my life because I never had before. Even in the ministry, I mostly worked and worked, and labored and struggled, feeling guilty most days because I focused on my faults and just generally was miserable. Finally I realized that Jesus really wanted me to have joy and enjoy my life (see John 10:10). Like anything else in the kingdom of God, joy is available, but holding on to it requires determination. The enemy will try his best to keep you from enjoying your life. Through his lies and deception he will try to make sure you don't have any peace, that you live under the burden of condemnation, and that you don't believe God loves you. Anytime you feel hopeless or joyless, realize immediately that what you feel is the devil at work, and you should resist him!

You can decide to enjoy your life—every aspect of it. Even in the midst of adverse circumstances or criticism from people you care about. You can be happy because your hope and your joy are based on God's goodness in your life, not the world's circumstances. When we live with hope and expectation that something good is about to happen, joy becomes our normal attitude.

> You can be happy because your hope and your joy are based on God's goodness in your life, not the world's circumstances.

The truth is that your circumstances will probably never change until your joy is no longer based on them changing. Let's be happy because of the hope we have in Jesus rather than being unhappy because we have a circumstance that we don't like.

The conditions in the world are always changing. It's easy to see why people are so unstable—because everything around them is unstable. Things are good one day but not so good the next. People may like you one day but may not like you the next. You've got a job one day but perhaps not the next. You have enough money one day, and then an unexpected expense leaves you in need. Your kids behave one day, but they've forgotten everything you ever taught them the next. If we are led by how we feel or the way things look, we will be emotional and unstable. The apostle James said we are often tossed hither and thither by the wind (James 1:6). The apostle Paul said we are like ships tossed about by changes (Ephesians 4:14). But we can be stable and unmoved by adversity or disappointment if we have hope as the anchor of our soul.

In a storm, one of the first things a ship does is drop anchor. The ship is tethered to something that is not moving. Everything around the sailors is moving, but they are not. They are anchored to the bottom of the ocean. Our hope in God can serve us in the same way. Everything around us is moving, but we are stable in Him.

Let Hope Soar

We want to let our hope in God be the anchor of our soul, instead of letting the cares and anxieties of the world weigh us down. Hope in God is an unfettered joy; it is not dragged down by the cares and burdens of the world. Think of a hot air balloon. As long as the balloon is held down by weights and tied down with ropes, it can't soar as it was created to do. The same is true for your life. If you allow the weight of worry to hold you down and the ropes of anxiety to bind you, you won't experience the life God created you to live. I want to encourage you to rid yourself of the baggage trying to weigh you down; being anchored in hope is very different from being weighed down by worry.

Here are a few things that try to weigh you down.

The Need to Be Like Other People

It was such a freeing lesson for me when I learned that I didn't have to be like other people. Our hope of acceptance can't be in trying to be someone we are not. God didn't create me to be like them. He created me to be me!

But before I realized that, I spent years trying to fit into someone else's mold. I tried to be easygoing like Dave, but that didn't last long. I tried to be quiet and soft-spoken like the pastor's wife at my church, and that was a disaster. I was so frustrated trying to be other people. But I wasn't supposed to be a copy of somebody else... and neither are you.

God created you to be you. And being content and comfortable with who He created you to be is essential if you are going to enjoy your life. Trying to be like your neighbor, or your co-worker, or the girl who sings onstage at church, or a Hollywood actor will only steal your joy. Don't compare yourself to someone else—enjoy who God created you to be.

Whether you realize it or not, you have unique gifts and talents. The Bible says you are "fearfully and wonderfully made" (Psalm 139:14 NIV). God crafted you into the person He wanted you to be. Nobody in the world is exactly like you—you are a one-of-a-kind masterpiece.

> Nobody in the world is exactly like you—you are a one-of-a-kind masterpiece.

Anytime you're tempted to think *Man, I wish I was more like this person* or *If only I had the talent of that person*, just realize they're probably saying the same things about someone else—maybe even you. We all face those feelings, but you don't have to let them weigh you down. Choose to be happy with who God made you to be, and let your soul be anchored in hope and let your joy soar.

Unforgiveness

When you choose to forgive the person who hurt or offended you, it's like cutting the rope that has been tying you down. Joy is restored to your life when you decide to forgive. When someone has hurt you, I suggest you do two things:

1. Decide to forgive in obedience to God's command.
2. Put your hope in God for justice to be done in your life. God promises to give us a double reward for our former trouble (Isaiah 61:7). Put your hope in that and expect reward!

When we hold on to grudges and unforgiveness, we're only hurting ourselves. The people who wounded us have gone on with their lives, not even thinking about what happened, and the whole time, we are allowing the poison of bitterness to ruin our lives. Don't allow a past hurt to hold you back another minute. Forgive the person who hurt you, give that wound to God, and ask Him to help you rise above the pain that has been so hard to let go.

A Hectic Pace of Life

If hope is going to be the anchor of your soul and joy your lifestyle, you may need to do a little pruning. You may have to simplify your life by trimming off the things that are not bearing any fruit. You may need to learn to say "no" to some things and not feel guilty about it. Keep your life light enough that joy can soar!

I'm speaking from experience. I used to complain all the time, saying "How can anybody keep up this pace? I need a vacation. I never get a break!" One day, I felt like the Lord was saying to me "If you don't want to do everything you're doing, just cut back. You're the one making the schedule." That was a freeing moment. I didn't have to try to do it all, and I didn't have to feel guilty about it. Think about this: Would God rather we be busy or joyful? I think we know the answer, so let's do what we can do without our activities becoming a burden to us.

Slow down and take time for the things that are really important. Spend time with your family and your friends. Enjoy your relationship with the Lord. Take time for yourself—enjoy a hobby.

Slowing down and enjoying your life is so important. If you're too busy to be happy, and if you're so busy you feel hopeless, it's time to make a change. Simplify your schedule and begin to really enjoy the life God has blessed you with.

There are countless things that can weigh us down. I have mentioned three, but I suggest you add to the list based on your own situations. Whether it's one of these three things or something else, refuse to let the lies of the enemy hold you down any longer.

The Best Source of Joy You'll Ever Find

Have you ever prayed and said, "Lord, I don't know what's wrong with me. I've lost my joy and I don't know what the problem is." Have you ever been so desperate to hear from God that you start looking at a Scripture calendar to see what it says for the day, or you flip your Bible open four or five times to see if you can get a Scripture that encourages you? Maybe watch a little Christian TV for a few minutes to see if you get some direction from the Lord?

One evening I was frantically searching for anything that would keep me from sinking into the despair I was feeling. I went to a stack of Scripture verses that were stored in a box in my kitchen and pulled out this one from Romans 15:13:

> *May the God of your hope so fill you with all joy and peace*
> *in believing [through the experience of your faith] that by the*
> *power of the Holy Spirit you may abound and be overflowing*
> *(bubbling over) with hope.*

I quickly realized that God was showing me that I had lost my joy because I had gotten negative and stopped being hopeful. Always believe in God and His promises! No matter what is happening, how bad it hurts or how long it lasts—always believe! If you do, you will be bubbling over with hope! That hope will be an anchor for your soul. Instead of being a baby Christian tossed about by every change, you will be a mature believer whom God can count on to represent Him well at all times.

Get Your Hopes Up!

Hope and happiness aren't things meant only for other people; they're things God wants you to experience in your life too. Don't let the enemy steal your joy. As a child of God, you've been given an abundance of blessings. Take time each day to realize how blessed you are and allow that realization to bring you joy.

There will be things in life that will try to weigh you down, keeping you from experiencing all God has for you. But you don't have to hold on to those weights or burdens for one more day. You can cast every care on the Lord and receive His joy in return. So go ahead and get your hopes up. Let hope be the anchor of your soul. It is a sure and a steadfast anchor, and it cannot break down under whoever steps out on it (Hebrews 6:19). Wow! What a promise.

HOPE IS HERE

. . . .

For You are my hope; O Lord God, You are my trust from my youth and the source of my confidence.

Psalm 71:5

"Now" is one of the most important words in the Bible. Jesus said, "I Am," and He meant I am here now. You don't have to look for Me at some other time! I am here! Hope is here!

What the world calls hope is not true hope at all. It is weak and vague, and is actually void of power. It always relegates everything good that might possibly happen some time in the future. Nothing is definite. Nothing is clear. Nothing is now!

As children of God, we have the privilege of believing that God is working *right now*, and that something good is happening in the spirit realm, and we will see it manifested very soon. In God's economy, we must believe first and then we will see. The world's kind of hope more or less vaguely "wishes" that things might change for the better, but there is no real hope, no real faith that it will happen until they see something that proves it.

Let's remember that Abraham had no visible reason to hope, but he hoped on in faith that he would have a child, as God had promised. He was "expecting" the good thing that God promised to happen. His expectation was real, and it was *now*.

In this section of the book, I want to help you live in the now, not in the past or the future. I want you to believe that right now, God is working in you and in your life.

> *Now faith is the assurance (the confirmation, the title deed)*
> *of the things [we] hope for, being the proof of things [we] do*
> *not see and the conviction of their reality [faith perceiving as*
> *real fact what is not revealed to the senses].*
>
> Hebrews 11:1

CHAPTER 14

Don't Wait for Tomorrow

*Behold, now is truly the time for a gracious welcome and
acceptance [of you from God]; behold, now is the day of
salvation!*

2 Corinthians 6:2

"Yesterday is history, tomorrow is a mystery, today is a
gift of God, which is why we call it the present."

—Bil Keane

Author Leo Buscaglia once told a story about his mother and what
he called their family "misery dinner." It was the night after his
father came home and said it looked as if he would have to go into
bankruptcy because his partner ran off with their firm's funds.
Buscaglia's mother went out and sold some jewelry to buy food for a
sumptuous feast. Other members of the family scolded her for sell-
ing the jewelry and for spending so much money. But she told them,
"The time for joy is now, when we need it most, not next week."[1]

I applaud the bold action and the wisdom of this mother. Hope and
joy are two things that should never be put off. Many people spend
their lives waiting for "tomorrow." They
say, "Well, maybe tomorrow things will
be better," or "I guess there's always
tomorrow," or "If I can just get through
this day and make it to tomorrow."

> Hope and joy are two
> things that should never
> be put off.

While they're putting off hope until tomorrow, they're not experiencing the joy of today, and that's not the life Jesus died to give us. Jesus
wants us to enjoy our lives today and every day.

Peace, joy, happiness, confidence, boldness, health, a sound mind,
favor, blessings, a strong marriage—these are all things God wants
you to begin experiencing today. Every time you think *Well, I guess
today is going to be a total waste; maybe tomorrow will be better*, you're
missing out on God's best plan for your life. If God is with you today—
and He is; He's always with you—you don't have to wait for some time
in the future to start rejoicing. You can experience His overcoming,
abundant, joy-filled life today. The apostle Paul said that while it is
still called TODAY, we should hear God and not harden our hearts
against His promises (Hebrews 3:15). God is working in your life *today*,
and He wants you to believe it *today* and to rejoice *today*!

Psalm 118:24 says, "**This** is the day which the Lord has brought
about; we will rejoice and be glad in it" (emphasis added). God
brought about this day for a reason. There is something special He
wants to do. Are you ready to receive it? Hopeful people do exactly
what that verse says: They rejoice and are glad. It doesn't matter
what the weather is outside, what they feel like, what others are
saying, how many odds are stacked against them, or what is happening in the news—people who have their hopes up say, "The
Lord brought about this day for a reason—I'm going to rejoice and
be glad. I'm going to have a happy anticipation that He is going to do
something good in my life today!"

Let me share a story about myself: In 1976, I had reached a place
of despair about the condition of my life. I thought that nothing good
would ever happen to me. Although I was a Christian, I was experiencing no victory in my life. While driving to work one morning in
February of that year, I cried out to God in desperation and I think
for the first time in my Christian walk I experienced what real faith
is. God put assurance in my heart that He was taking care of my

situation. Although nothing changed immediately in my circumstance, after that I had total peace. I was filled with the happy anticipation that something good was going to happen that day. I had real hope! It didn't matter to me what God did, or even when He did it, because in my heart I knew it was done. I can honestly say that from that moment on, things started changing in my life. They were not perfect by any means, but little by little, day after day, good things happened.

I know this question may be in your mind: "Joyce, what if I believe something good will happen today and it doesn't?" First of all, let me say that I firmly believe something good does happen every day, but we may not see it. Second, the good that takes place may not be exactly what we hoped for, but hope gave us a better day than we would have had without it, so that alone is a good thing. And last, I will say that you should get up again tomorrow with hope, believing something good will happen to you that day. No matter how many days you have to do it, keep doing it, and you will see that God is faithful!

Consistency Is the Key

A lack of consistency is one of our biggest failings. One of the reasons why many people can seem to experience great victory on some days but crushing defeat on others is because of their own daily inconsistencies. You'd be amazed at what a difference it can make in your life if you will make the decision to be consistent each day. It is not what we do right one time that changes our lives but what we do right consistently! If you are hopeful one day and not the next, you won't like the results. If you believe that what I am teaching you about hope is true, and you decide to live filled with it, then make a decision to do it consistently. We do what is right because it is right! We are committed!

Let Go of the Balloon

I once heard about a conference that was being held in a church auditorium. People were given helium-filled balloons and told to release them at some point in the service when they felt like expressing the joy in their hearts. Throughout the service balloons ascended to the high, vaulted ceiling at various times, but when the service was over, a third of the balloons had yet to be released.

Isn't that amazing? A third of the people in that crowd waited so long that they missed their chance to join in the celebration and let go of their balloon. As children of God who have the opportunity to live full of hope and joy, we don't have to wait for some time in the future to enjoy the life God has given us—we can enjoy it right now.

So many people have the mind-set that they will be really happy and enjoy life *when*. *When* they go on vacation, *when* they get married, *when* they get higher on the ladder of success at work, *when* they have a baby, *when* they make more money, *when* the kids get older, *when* their spouse treats them better—you get the picture.

I can relate to this because there was a time when even though I really loved being in the ministry, I wasn't always enjoying the daily responsibilities and activities it involved. I had to learn to live in the moment and enjoy what God was doing in me and through me *now*, not *when* the conference was over, or *when* the project was completed, or *when* I could go on vacation. God showed me the importance of embracing and enjoying what He was doing in the present.

The same is true for you. There will always be a *when* in your life. The kids might be driving you crazy today, your boss might be in a bad mood today, your body may ache today, your emotions might be out of whack today, but none of that changes the fact that God is with you in this very moment and He has a good plan for your life…and today is part of that plan.

Making the Most of Today

Psalm 71:14 says, "But I will hope continually, and will praise You yet more and more." The key word in this verse about hope is "continually." A hopeful person doesn't hope *occasionally* or *sporadically*. And a hopeful person certainly doesn't wait until tomorrow to expect something good from God. A hopeful person is *continually* hopeful, choosing to hope every day...all throughout the day.

> *A hopeful person is continually hopeful, choosing to hope every day...all throughout the day.*

Let me suggest a few ways you can live in continual hope, making every day a day filled with the happy anticipation of good.

Pray One Bold Prayer Each Day

If you have hope, you're never afraid to believe big. In fact, I like to say that hope is the platform that faith stands on. That's why it's a good idea to go to God with a bold prayer today. You can't live with an expectation today if you haven't even had the faith to make a request.

Whatever it is that's in your heart, if it lines up with the Word of God, dare to ask confidently and then wait expectantly. God loves bold prayers. He answered them time and time again in the Bible, and He still answers them today. Exercise hope, stand in faith, and ask Him for something bold and do it NOW!

Do Something Fun Each Day

Sometimes we lose our hope simply because we lose our joy. Instead of enjoying life every day, we get burned-out by bills and discouraged by dilemmas. Why not decide to do something fun each day? It doesn't have to be a daily trip to Disney World. It could be as simple as coffee with a friend, watching a comedy with your family, or a walk in the park—anything that brings a smile to your face.

If you want to be continually full of hope, plan fun things that will create a sense of anticipation. Hope and joy go together, so plan something fun and go through your day enjoying God's presence and every blessing He gives you.

We all need fun and enjoyable things to look forward to. Today I am writing for several hours. I also plan to go for coffee with some friends later today, do a little shopping, and go out to dinner tonight. When I plan my day, I always include something that I can look forward to. Don't wait until you retire to think about enjoying life. Enjoy life NOW!

Bless at Least One Person Each Day

I love looking around and finding people I can bless. It's such a blessing to bless others! If you really want to enjoy your day, I suggest you help someone else enjoy theirs. Maybe you can buy someone's lunch, give an encouraging compliment, or tell someone they are important to you and that you appreciate them.

Ask God to show you how you can be a blessing and then follow His instruction. As you look to meet the needs of others, you're going to be surprised at how easy it becomes to hope and believe that God is going to meet your needs as well. Don't put off being a blessing. Do it today! Be a blessing NOW!

Write Down at Least One Way Each Day
That God Blessed You

Hope thrives in an atmosphere of thankfulness. If you want to live with hope on a continual basis, spend each day looking for ways the Lord has blessed you. You're going to be surprised at the number of things you'll find. The more you realize how God is blessing you NOW, the more hopeful you will be that you will see even greater things.

At the end of each day, take a moment to write those things down. Start a "testimony of hope" journal. Some days you might have one or two things to jot down, other days you might have 10 or 20 things, filling an entire page. Start documenting God's goodness in your life and watch how easy it is to never live one day without vibrant hope.

Get Your Hopes Up!

Let hope rise up now. You don't have to wait days, weeks, months, or years to expect God to move. He's with you, and He's already moving in your life. Pray for greater awareness so you never fail to see what God is doing in your life.

There will always be a temptation to live in the procrastination of *when* rather than the power of *now*. Don't let the difficulties of the day talk you into putting off your anticipation of God's goodness. Go ahead and get your hopes up. Something great could happen today. A breakthrough could take place today. Don't wait until tomorrow to believe it—believe it today.

> There will always be a temptation to live in the procrastination of when rather than the power of now.

CHAPTER 15

Get God's Perspective

*[Most] blessed is the man who believes in, trusts in, and
relies on the Lord, and whose hope and confidence the
Lord is.*

Jeremiah 17:7

"God is the only one who can make the valley of trouble
a door of hope."

—Catherine Marshall

Sometimes you just don't know how things can possibly work out.
Have you ever felt that way before? You're reading your Bible every
day, you're trying to keep a positive attitude, you have good friends
who are encouraging you to hang in there, but try as you might,
you're still discouraged. You just aren't experiencing the kind of
hope we've been talking about so far in this book. Sure, you may
have some days that are more hopeful than others, but you wouldn't
consider yourself a hopeful person.

You're not the only one who has felt that way. Many people struggle to find hope—and many more struggle to hang on to hope. Hope
cannot be based on your circumstances; it must be founded on
Christ alone. Hope doesn't just show up because you wish it would.
Hope is something that has to be nurtured and developed, and regular study of God's Word is the fuel needed to feed it. You don't
have to wait—hope is here. You can begin receiving hope today. You

don't have to wait to feel it, but you can simply make a decision that life is miserable without hope so why not be hopeful NOW! Expect something good to happen today!

One of the most important things you can do to live a life of hope—a life filled with the happy anticipation of good—is to get God's perspective. As long as you are seeing the situations in your life through a natural, fleshly perspective, you are going to be tempted to feel helpless and defeated. But when you begin to see your life the way that God sees it, hope takes over.

This is what happened with Abraham. In Genesis chapter 15, Abraham was feeling pretty hopeless. God had made promises that Abraham would be a father of many nations (see Genesis 12:2) and that the land of Canaan would go to his posterity (see Genesis 12:5–7), but Abraham just didn't see how things could work out. He loved God, and he wanted to have hope, but he had no children. How was God going to make him into a great nation if Abraham didn't even have an heir?

In Genesis 15:2–3, Abraham prayed one of those honest prayers we all pray from time to time. He said, "Lord God, what can You give me, since I am going on [from this world] childless?..." And Abraham continued, "Look, You have given me no child...." Abraham was frustrated. He was looking at things from his perspective, and his perspective wasn't offering much hope.

Knowing that Abraham wasn't seeing the big picture, God did something amazing. Genesis 15:5 says:

> *And He brought him outside [his tent into the starlight] and said, Look now toward the heavens and count the stars—if you are able to number them. Then He said to him, So shall your descendants be.*

In the middle of Abraham's pity party, God knew what Abraham needed—he needed a change in perspective. There he was, hopelessly praying to God about the small picture—one descendant—and all the while God was planning to bless him with descendants too numerous to count. So God brought him outside and gave Abraham a new perspective: a sky full of stars. The moment Abraham got God's perspective, his hope came alive. Romans 4:18 (NIV) says: "Against all hope, Abraham in hope believed and so became the father of many nations, just as it had been said to him, 'So shall your offspring be.'"

Abraham's story is so encouraging. It tells me that even the best of us can get discouraged from time to time. It's natural to question God when we can't see how the promise could possibly come true. But we don't have to stay stuck in those feelings of doubt and discouragement. God wants to give us His perspective in order to fill us with hope and faith. Rather than looking at the small picture, God wants to show us the big picture—*His* picture—because His perspective changes everything.

> *Rather than looking at the small picture, God wants to show us the big picture—His picture—because His perspective changes everything.*

Put on Your God Glasses

Let's put on what I will call our "God glasses," and look at some things from God's perspective. He sees things very differently than we do because He sees the end from the beginning.

How does God see you? He loves you more than you will ever understand, and He has a good plan for your life. You are never alone because He is with you all the time. God's forgiveness is greater than any sin you have committed. His mercy is new every day. God has given you, as a believer, power, and you do not have to live a defeated life. You have been made brand-new in Christ, given a new life, and you can let go of all that is behind you and look forward to the things that are ahead. When you know who you are in Christ—and how God views you because of the sacrifice of His Son—it will change the way you live.

God looked at creation and said it was good (see Genesis 1:31). You're part of creation, so you're good. But we may have a hard time believing that. I'm not talking about your flesh. The apostle Paul said, "Nothing good dwells within me, that is, in my flesh." (Romans 7:18). Our flesh is flawed, and we all make mistakes. When God says "You're good," He's talking about the newly re-created spiritual you!

> *For we are God's [own] handiwork (His workmanship), re-created in Christ Jesus, [born anew] that we may do those good works which God predestined (planned beforehand) for us...that we should walk in them [living the good life which He prearranged and made ready for us to live].*
>
> Ephesians 2:10

It is very important that we understand the new creation realities and begin to identify with them. A lot of people act badly because they think they're bad—they *believe* they're bad. People often stay stuck in a sinful lifestyle because they don't believe they have been set free from it through Christ. They look at what they've always been and they don't understand the real power of the new birth—that if any man be in Christ, he is a new creature, old things have passed away, and all things have become brand-new (see 2 Corinthians 5:17).

As difficult as it is to understand or to truly believe, God now views us as righteous through Jesus.

> *For our sake He made Christ [virtually] to be sin Who knew no sin, so that in and through Him we might become [endued with, viewed as being in, and examples of] the righteousness of God [what we ought to be, approved and acceptable and in right relationship with Him, by His goodness].*
>
> 2 Corinthians 5:21

As someone who felt "wrong" most of my life, learning about the doctrine of righteousness through Christ was and is amazingly freeing and wonderful to me. I love to help people understand this so they can stop rejecting themselves because they can't seem to be perfect on a daily basis. Our right standing with God is not based on what we do, but it is based on what Jesus has done.

As we learn more and more about the love, acceptance, and grace of God, we notice that hope becomes our continual companion. I honestly cannot recall the last time I felt hopeless! We can learn to trust God and to always have confidence that as we are growing and changing, God sees our love and commitment to Him and still views us as being in right relationship with Him.

There is a big difference between who you are and what you do. That's why I encourage people to separate their "who" from their "do." You are a child of God. You are born again. You are filled with His Spirit. Instead of looking at your flesh, get God's perspective and look at your spirit. See yourself in the mirror of the Word of God, and then get excited about who you are in Christ Jesus.

I urge you to also get God's perspective on your trials. See them the way God does. He sees that they are temporary. No problem lasts forever, so keep your hopes up because your breakthrough is closer than you think. When you look through your God glasses, you will have to say "This won't last forever and I will outlast it!"

> When you get into a tight place and everything goes against you till it seems as though you could not hold on a minute longer, never give up then, for that is just the place and time that the tide will turn.
>
> —Harriet Beecher Stowe

God desires that you go all the way through with Him. Going on or giving up is our choice. God gives us His promise, but it is up to us to stand steadfast and wait out every storm in life. Of course God helps us. He gives us His grace, His strength, and His encourage-ment, but, ultimately, we must decide to press on or to quit. One of the benefits of trials is that God uses them to harden us to difficulty.

> *Fear not [there is nothing to fear], for I am with you; do not look around you in terror and be dismayed, for I am your God. I will strengthen and harden you to difficulties...*
>
> Isaiah 41:10a

This is an awesome Scripture that tells us that even when we go through something difficult, God will work something good out of it. He does many things, but one is that He makes us stronger. We are hardened to difficulties. In other words, things that once upset us, or frightened or worried us, won't bother us at all.

A person who works out at the gym with weights will get muscle, but once he or she reaches a certain point, the only way to get more muscle is to lift heavier weights. When we ask God for promotion in any area of our life, we can expect God to do something in us before He can do something for us. We might say that we have to become accustomed to lifting heavier weights in the spirit.

For example, we may pray that our love abound more and more, but that may also mean that we will be around more people who are difficult to love. I remember one time praying for the ability to love the unlovely! A couple of weeks later, I was murmuring to God in prayer about the difficult people who had come my way, and He reminded me that I could not learn to love the unlovely if I was only around lovely people who never irritated me in any way.

When we pray for God to use us in greater ways, we should remember that Paul said that a wide door of opportunity had opened for him, and with it came many adversaries (1 Corinthians 16:9). Satan opposes anything good. He hates growth and progress of any kind, but if we remain steadfast, God will deliver us and simultane-ously He will help us grow spiritually through the difficulty.

This doesn't mean that God is the author of our problems, but He certainly does use them to help us in many ways. When you are in the midst of a challenging or painful situation, try to think of the good that can come from it, instead of merely how hard it is. When all reason for hope is gone, hope on in faith, as Abraham did.

From God's perspective, good things are happening even while you are waiting for your breakthrough or deliverance. You are growing spiritually, you are developing patience, you are enduring a test, and when you pass it you will experience promotion. And you are glorifying God by loving Him the same now as you will when your circumstance changes.

Trials are valuable. They hurt, but they are valuable! We all go through them, but we don't all go through them successfully. I often say that after a test, some people have a testimony, but others only have the "moanies."

Making Hope a Habit

In order to get God's perspective, you may need to develop some new routines in your daily life—some new habits. Hearing the word "habits" might cause you to think of bad habits (because bad habits get most of the attention these days), but you can develop good habits too. Most notably, you can make hope a habit. Hope can be something you develop over time until it just becomes your natural disposition.

> You can make hope a habit.

An attitude of expectancy—looking, longing, and anticipating that God is going to do something great—isn't something that will always come naturally to you. This is a mind-set of hope that you're going to have to intentionally develop until it becomes second nature…a habit. One of the ways to do this is to remind yourself to be expectant of good things. Maybe you should put signs up all over your house that remind you to have a hopeful heart. I believe in employing all methods necessary when I am working on developing a new habit. Good habits leave no room for bad ones, so if we have a habit of hope, there will be no room in our mind and heart for hopelessness, discouragement, and despair.

Habakkuk 2:2 says:

And the Lord answered me and said, Write the vision and engrave it so plainly upon tablets that everyone who passes may [be able to] read [it easily and quickly] as he hastens by.

Write your vision down. It doesn't have to be anything long or elaborate. You could make small signs that can be read "easily and quickly" as you and your family hasten by. Think of how much more hopeful you would be if...

- When you get up to brush your teeth, there's a sign on the bathroom mirror that reads: "Hope is important. Don't forget to believe God is going to do something great in your life today."
- When you walk down the hall, there's a sign that reads: "Hope is the happy anticipation of good. Get happy. God has good things in store."
- When you go into the kitchen to make breakfast, there's a sign above the stove that reads: "Get excited. God is cooking up something amazing today."
- When you get in the car to go to work, take the kids to school, or meet a friend for coffee, there's a sign that reads: "Get your hopes up. God is with you today, and He delights in being good to you."

I don't know about you, but I'm getting hopeful already! If you want to live a life of hope, do whatever it takes. There are a lot of things during your day that try to steal your hope. Decide you're going to outnumber the "hope stealers" with reminders of hope.

Plaster them everywhere! This is especially important if you have had a tendency to be negative or depressed, or if you are going through a particularly difficult time.

The Higher You Go, the Better You See

I have to admit, I'm not much of a hiker. You may be, but it's not really my cup of tea. I'd much rather spend a weekend hanging out with my kids than exploring forest or mountain trails. But I've been told that when hikers get turned around and they're trying to figure out exactly where they are, they look to go higher. A higher vantage point gives them a better perspective. Whether they have to climb a tree, scurry up a hill, or scale a large boulder, hikers go higher. They've learned that the higher they go, the farther they can see.

I think the same is true for you and me today. Sometimes it's hard to see where we're going because we have limited vision. We can get confused by our surroundings and unsure where to go next because we don't have the right perspective. Our hope and direction are diminished by a canopy of past failures, a fog of low expectations, and canyons of despair.

In order to get God's perspective, you need to go higher. You hike past ingratitude; you climb above doubt and discouragement. If you'll choose higher expectations and higher hopes, I believe you're going to start to get a new perspective—a godly perspective. And when that happens, you're going to be able to see farther than you ever have before.

Get Your Hopes Up!

You can determine what kind of life you are going to live based on the way you choose to look at yourself and the situations in your life. If you look at your faults and failures, thinking those are the things that define you, you're not going to hope that God will do much in your life. And if you look at and talk about your problems constantly, they're going to seem too big to overcome, and you're going to find that hope is a hard thing to hold on to.

But thankfully, there is a different perspective. God's perspective for you and for your life is a better perspective...and it is the only one that really matters. When God looks at you, He is full of love, and He has already put together a great plan for your life. Jeremiah 29:11 (NIV) says, "'For I know the plans I have for you,' declares the Lord, 'plans to prosper you and not to harm you, plans to give you hope and a future.'" So go ahead and get your hopes up. God has blessed you in the past, and He promises to bless you in the future. Any time you're not sure how it's all going to work out, just go outside at night and look up at the stars. God kept His promise to Abraham, and He's going to keep His promises to you too.

CHAPTER 16

The Choice Is Yours

*Do not be anxious about anything, but in every situation,
by prayer and petition, with thanksgiving, present your
requests to God. And the peace of God, which transcends
all understanding, will guard your hearts and your minds
in Christ Jesus.*

Philippians 4:6–7 (NIV)

"Hope is the power of being cheerful in circumstances
which we know to be desperate."

—G. K. Chesterton

It's wonderful to know that hope is here—it's available to you and to
me today. But in order to live in the reality of that truth, there is an
enemy of hope we will need to defeat: worry.

Worry is a bitter foe of hope. It's impossible to be full of hope and
full of worry at the same time. You have to choose one, because the
two are diametrically opposed. Hope
sees all the good things that can happen; worry manifests as evil forebod-
ings. It is concerned that something
bad may happen. Worry and fear work
hand in hand, and leave us thinking that if we can just figure out
what to do about our situation, perhaps we can put an end to the
difficulty. And even though the Bible tells us repeatedly that worry

> It's impossible to be
> full of hope and full of
> worry at the same time.

is useless and not to do it, it is one of the greatest temptations we deal with. Making the transition from trusting in our own selves to solve our problems and totally trusting in God to do it takes time.

I came across an illustrated story that demonstrates the key to overcoming worry and living in the fullness of hope...

A pastor had been on a long flight from one place to another. The first warning of the approaching problems came when the sign on the airplane flashed on: "Fasten your seat belts." Then, after a while, a calm voice said, "We shall not be serving the beverages at this time as we are expecting a little turbulence. Please be sure your seat belt is fastened."

As the pastor looked around the aircraft, it became obvious that many of the passengers were getting anxious. Later, the flight attendant said, "We are so sorry that we are unable to serve the meal at this time. The turbulence is still ahead of us." And then the storm broke. The ominous cracks of thunder could be heard even above the roaring sound of the engines. Lightning lit up the darkening skies, and within moments, that great plane was like a cork tossed around on a celestial ocean. One moment the airplane was lifted on terrific currents of air, the next, it dropped as if it were about to crash.

The pastor confessed that he shared the discomfort and fear of those around him. He said, "As I looked around the plane, I could see that nearly all the passengers were upset and alarmed. Some were praying. The future seemed ominous and many were wondering if they would make it through the storm. Then I suddenly saw a little girl. Apparently the storm meant nothing to her. She tucked her feet beneath her as she sat on her seat; she was reading a book, and everything within her small world was calm and orderly. Sometimes she closed her eyes, then she would read again; then she would straighten her legs, but worry and fear were not in her world. When the plane was being buffeted by the terrible storm, when it lurched this way and that, as it rose and fell with frightening severity, when all the adults were scared half to death, that marvelous child was completely composed and unafraid."

The minister could hardly believe his eyes. It was not surprising, therefore, when the plane finally reached its destination and all the passengers were hurrying to disembark, our pastor lingered to speak to the girl whom he had watched for such a long time. After commenting about the storm and behavior of the plane, he asked why she had not been afraid.

The child replied, "'Cause my daddy's the pilot, and he's taking me home."[1]

What a great illustration of how to find peace, even in the midst of the storm. This little girl was never afraid or anxious because she trusted that her dad knew what he was doing. Everyone else was focused on the storm around them, panicking and worrying that they weren't going to make it. But those thoughts never occurred to this little girl. In her mind, her dad was in total control the whole time—she didn't have anything to worry about.

If you want to overcome worry in your life, I encourage you to take on the same attitude. Instead of assuming the worst whenever things get difficult, have the faith to sit back and relax. There might be some turbulence, and the people around you might show signs of fear, but you know something they might not know…your Heavenly Father is the pilot. There's no way He is going to let you go down. He's been in control the whole time.

> Instead of assuming the worst whenever things get difficult, have the faith to sit back and relax.

Calm in the Storm

Romans 8:24–25 says this about hope:

> *For in [this] hope we were saved. But hope [the object of]*
> *which is seen is not hope. For how can one hope for what*
> *he already sees?* **But if we hope for what is still unseen**
> **by us, we wait for it with patience and composure.**
> (*emphasis added*)

What is composure? It means our emotions are under control. When somebody gets emotionally distraught, you might say to them, "Compose yourself." The Bible teaches that hope will allow us to wait on God with an attitude of patience and composure. In other words, while we're waiting on God, we can remain calm. We won't be frantic and fearful, and even if we are tempted in that way, we can overcome it by remembering that God loves us and will not leave us forsaken. Don't merely "try" not to be upset, but, instead, face the worrisome thoughts with reminders of how God has delivered you in the past, and know that He will do it again. We may be struck down, but we are never struck out!

Hope brings a level of peaceful calm and composure. Hope says, "I don't see the answer to my situation yet with my natural eyes, but by faith I believe that God is working." Always remember that worry is a total waste of energy. It wears us out mentally and emotionally and does absolutely no good. Worry changes nothing except us! It confuses us when we frantically search in our mind for answers to problems that only God has answers for. God is not the author of confusion, He is the Prince of Peace. He wants you to live in hope so that even on days when it seems like everything around you is spinning out of control, you can be firm in your belief that something good is going to happen. Believe it, meditate on it, speak it, and encourage others who are also facing trials.

Imagine a set of parents sitting at their son's soccer game. One of these parents is a chronic worrier, and the other is not. The worrying parent assumes the worst; the other parent believes for the best.

Now, their son is in second grade—and he's running around, kicking the ball, and having a great time. All of a sudden, he turns around, runs into an opposing player, falls down, and scrapes his knee. This, of course, causes the normal shedding of a few tears, and all the other kids wait while the scraped knee is attended to. Both parents look intently onto the field to make sure their son is okay (which he is), but their outlook on life causes them to have drastically different reactions.

The parent who lives with patience and composure watches carefully as the coach goes out to check on the child. This parent has a level of concern, as any parent would, but when it's apparent the boy is merely in need of a Band-Aid and some orange wedges, this parent gives an enthusiastic thumbs-up and encourages the boy to enjoy the rest of the game. This optimistic parent isn't unaware of the situation but refuses to be unsettled and unnerved just because there is a possibility of an injury. There is a healthy and happy anticipation of good rather than an unhealthy and miserable dread that something bad is going to happen.

The worrying parent has a completely different reaction. This parent charges the field wildly. Before the coach, or even the referee, can check to see if the boy is all right, the worrying parent is already there, frantically examining the knee and wondering how much the hospital bill is going to cost. Keep in mind, it's just a scraped knee, but a worrier has very little composure. This parent makes a big scene, carrying the boy off the field, rushing to the car, imagining the child in a cast and with crutches.

Maybe you've witnessed scenes like this play out in the lives of people around you (or maybe in your own life). People who fall apart at the first sign of trouble often say, "Well, I'm just a worrier," excusing their reactions like it's just a personality trait. But worry is a weapon of the enemy meant to steal your joy and the joy of all those around you. It's not a personality quirk; it is based on fear and a failure to trust in God.

You don't have to go through life fearing the worst. You don't have to become frantic and get out of control emotionally with every scraped knee. You can live with a hopeful assurance that things are going to be okay. In fact, they're going to be better than okay—they're going to be great! God is in control, and when you trust His plan for your life, hope, peace, and composure will be the natural results. None of this means that we won't have to deal with unpleasant circumstances, or that everything in life will be the way we would like it to be, but it does mean that we can choose to believe the best or to believe the worst—it is up to us!

The Calming Effect of Hope

People, including Christians, can have a big problem with a lack of stability—and that lack of stability comes because of worry and fear. Worry causes people to be up and down emotionally, and their minds may run wild with erratic thoughts. You never know what you're going to encounter with family members or friends who tend to worry. Their emotions are based on the events of the day, so they are unpredictable and unreliable. They don't mean to be this way; this is just what worry does. They would like to be calm, but they mistakenly think that the only way they can be calm is if all their circumstances are pleasant.

I spent many years in emotional ups and downs, and I prayed constantly for God to fix my problems so I could be peaceful. Now I know that God's goal for us is that we are peaceful in the storm as Jesus was. Why doesn't God just remove our problems? After all, He could if He wanted to. The answer is simply that we are in the world, and in the world there will be tribulation (John 16:33). To never have any difficulty, we would have to get out of the world altogether. For now this is where we are. Being here is not always easy, but God has equipped us with everything we need to stay calm and enjoy life no matter what.

Be Realistic

I am encouraging you in every chapter of this book to expect good things, but that doesn't mean that we should have unrealistic expectations. It is unrealistic to expect people to be perfect and never hurt you, or to expect that every day of your life things will be exactly as you want them to be. Believing that good things are going to happen will help you navigate the storms of life and still arrive at your destination. We go through things, but thank God that we "go through." Going through may not be pleasant, but it sure is better than staying stuck and never making it through.

I don't wake up expecting problems, but I am aware that they may come, and I have already set my mind to stay full of hope and have a positive expectation that things will work out for good! We are more than conquerors, and to me that means we can have assurance of victory even before we have a problem. "Victorious" becomes our new identity! We don't need to live with a victim mentality because we are assured that in the end, we always win!

Being fully convinced of these things allows us to be stable and calm. In 1 Corinthians 15:58, the apostle Paul says that we can be "firm (steadfast), immovable, always abounding in the work of the Lord." What a great description of what it means to follow Jesus. This is exactly how a person who has made God the foundation of his life can live. "Firm," "steadfast," and "immovable" are characteristics we develop as a result of setting worry aside and consistently deciding to live in hope.

Hope brings strength and stability to your life. When you have confidence that God is in control and He is going to do something great in your situation, you're not tossed around wildly by the storms of life; instead, you are anchored and secure because your hope is in the Lord.

Which Are You: Vulture or Hummingbird?

An article in *Reader's Digest* said:

> Both the hummingbird and the vulture fly over our nation's deserts. All vultures see is rotting meat, because that is what they look for. They thrive on that diet. But hummingbirds ignore the smelly flesh of dead animals. Instead, they look for the colorful blossoms of desert plants. The vultures live on what was. They live on the past. They fill themselves with what is dead and gone. But hummingbirds live on what is. They seek new life. They fill themselves with freshness and life. Each bird finds what it is looking for. We all do.[2]

The difference between the vulture and the hummingbird is a lot like the difference between worry and hope. Like the vulture, worry feeds on things that have no life: negativity, pessimism, fear, anxiety. It's an ugly way to live, savaging for sustenance among dead and dying things. But hope is different. Like the hummingbird, hope is beautiful. Hope seeks new life, feeding on what is fresh and new.

> *The difference between the vulture and the hummingbird is a lot like the difference between worry and hope.*

As a child of God, it is your right to enjoy your life, but in order to do that, you will need to choose to be positive, looking for what is fresh and new. Being positive means that you're actively looking for good things. You're constantly believing and searching for the good things God has for you, not looking for or anticipating the next disaster.

It's not enough to just get rid of negativity—that's just the beginning. You have the opportunity to get rid of negativity...and then embrace a positive outlook on life!

I remember when God dealt with me strongly about the effects of negativity and challenged me to stop thinking and speaking negative things. I went a few months and thought I was really doing well, but I still didn't see any positive changes in my circumstances. As I pondered the situation, I sensed God showing me that although I had greatly improved in not being so negative, I had failed to begin being positive. God wants us to not only stop doing wrong things, but He also wants us to do the right things. The apostle Paul taught that the thief should steal no more but work so he could help others in need. He said we should avoid anger and resentment and instead be kind to everybody, doing what is for their benefit (Ephesians 4:28, 31–32).

God wants to replace the worldly principles with godly principles. You see it all throughout the Bible. He takes our sin, and He gives us His righteousness. He takes our turmoil, and He gives us His peace. He takes our sadness, and He gives us His joy. He removes the bad thing, and He brings in the good thing.

Here's what it might look like in your life...

- Maybe you stopped mistreating someone. That's a good step. But now take another step and start being good to them, blessing them every chance you get.
- Maybe you stopped saying bad things about people, but now you might need to be aggressive in finding good things to say about them.
- Maybe you stopped complaining all the time about the tough things in your life. That's a good step. But now take another step and start being thankful for the good things you experience each day.

- Maybe you stopped assuming you were going to have a terrible day in the morning when you wake up. That's a good step. But now take another step and start assuming you're going to have a great day in God.

As I mentioned in the last chapter, the Bible says that God looked at creation and "it was very good" (Genesis 1:31). I love how God took time to recognize and appreciate the good. I think we should do the same thing. Let's choose to be hummingbirds, not vultures. Let's put aside the negative things and go in search of the things that are good. I don't know about you, but I'd rather be a hummingbird than a vulture.

Get Your Hopes Up!

If you've dealt with worry or anxiety in your life, this could be a moment of breakthrough for you. You can decide to live your life full of hope in God, excited and optimistic about His plan for your life. Worry isn't part of your DNA. It's an enemy that you can defeat with the Lord's help.

When difficult situations arise, you don't have to panic and fall apart; you can be full of peace and composure. The Lord is your Rock, and He will anchor you so that you're not tossed around by the storms of life. So go ahead and get your hopes up. You can be a hummingbird, not a vulture. You can see the good in every situation rather than the bad. And if you come across a storm and the turbulence has you feeling afraid, don't worry...your Heavenly Father is your pilot!

CHAPTER 17

Let Hope Overflow

May the God of your hope so fill you with all joy and peace in believing [through the experience of your faith] that by the power of the Holy Spirit you may abound and be overflowing (bubbling over) with hope.

Romans 15:13

"Joy runs deeper than despair."

—Corrie ten Boom

All You Can Eat!

I carefully considered how to begin the last chapter of this book, but I kept coming back to those four words: ALL YOU CAN EAT! I've written over 100 books, but I can safely say I've never begun a chapter like this.

"All you can eat" is something you may not indulge in often, but you probably make the most of it when you do. Recently someone I know told me that he takes his family to an all-you-can-eat buffet every Thanksgiving—it's their family tradition. Instead of cooking all morning and cleaning dishes all evening, they go to the same restaurant each Thanksgiving holiday and enjoy the buffet. Trip after trip to the counter for more turkey—plate after plate of potatoes, stuffing, green beans, yams, and cranberry sauce. And for this special occasion, he and his wife let the kids go to the dessert bar as many times as they want. He said, "Joyce, we only go out for 'all you can eat' once a year, but when we do, we definitely get our money's worth!"

I mention this as we begin our last chapter together because I think hope is an item on God's All-You-Can-Eat Buffet menu. It's not the only dish He offers, but it's a prominent one. Grace, hope, love, forgiveness, acceptance, strength, safety—these are just a few of the things God offers with no limitations. You can never go back for grace too many times. You'll never exhaust the Father's supply of love. It's impossible to ask for too much hope.

> It's impossible to ask for too much hope.

Whatever you're believing God for today—whether it's regarding your family, your emotional health, your physical health, your relationships, your career, your finances, your future—take the limits off. Go back to the buffet and fill up on hope as many times as it takes. When people talk about you, they should say, "That's a person overflowing with hope. No matter what happens, no matter what it looks like around them, they never give up on God."

Look at your soul as a glass; don't let it be just a quarter full of hope. Don't settle for halfway full of hope. Three-quarters of the way full of hope isn't enough. You can even do better than being full of hope—let hope spill over, splash everywhere, and get all over other people. Choose to overflow with hope in God. Believe He is going to do exceedingly and abundantly more than you can even ask or think (see Ephesians 3:20).

God of More Than Enough

One of the things we know about Jesus is that He likes to exceed expectations. There is no doubting His power, because He does more than give us what we need; He gives us what we need...plus some. Here is a Scripture that positively confirms this principle:

And God is able to make all grace (every favor and earthly blessing) come to you in abundance, so that you may always and under all circumstances and whatever the need be self-sufficient [possessing enough to require no aid or support and furnished in abundance for every good work and charitable donation].

2 Corinthians 9:8

God promises enough for you and an overflow besides so you can help other people. This sounds like an exciting way to live, and I sure don't want to miss it—do you?

In John chapter 6, we find the familiar story of Jesus feeding the crowd of 5,000 (plus the women and children). The disciples were panicked because the crowd was hungry, and there was no way they had enough food to feed all these people. A hungry mob and helpless disciples—this did not look good.

Can you relate to that feeling of helplessness? Have you ever been in a situation where the problem was so big you knew there was no way you could fix it on your own?

- Your marriage is suffering, but you have no idea how to fix it.
- You feel lonely and discouraged, but you have no idea how to fix it.
- You've fallen out of favor at work, but you have no idea how to fix it.
- Your income isn't enough to cover your bills, but you have no idea how to fix it.
- Your kids are struggling at school, but you have no idea how to fix it.

This may be how the disciples felt. People were looking to them, but they felt hopeless. Their problem was too big, and their abilities were too small. So they did the only thing they could do—they went to Jesus. The Word of God tells us Jesus took the very little they had (five barley loaves of bread and two small fish), He prayed over it, and then He began to multiply it.

At first, the disciples probably assumed it would only feed two or three people. But the supply kept coming from the hands of the Savior. Ten people were fed, 100 people were fed, 500 people were fed, 1,000 people were fed. To their amazement, the provisions kept coming and coming and coming! And the most incredible part of the story isn't just that everyone was fed—everyone was fed until they were full and satisfied . . . and there were still 12 baskets of food left over. Jesus provided more than enough.

ALL YOU CAN EAT!

If Jesus could satisfy a hungry crowd, just imagine what He can do for your hungry soul. Whatever you are going through today, it's no match for the power of God in your life. There is no reason for you to be worried or afraid—

> *If Jesus could satisfy a hungry crowd, just imagine what He can do for your hungry soul.*

hope is here. The same Jesus who provided so much food that there were 12 baskets left over—He's providing for you too.

Don't hesitate to believe and to ask God to do the unthinkable and unimaginable in your life. One of God's favorite things is to take something that is thought to be impossible and turn it into amazing possibilities. When the sea gets in the way of His people's escape, He parts the sea. When the sun starts to go down during a victory, He tells the sun to stand still. When a restless crowd gets hungry, He feeds them from a lunchbox. Every time He moves, there is victory, daylight, and food to spare. So don't ask God for barely enough; try asking Him for too much. Don't ask with a selfish motive or you may get nothing, but if you want more than enough so you can be a blessing to hurting and needy people, you can expect exceedingly, abundantly, above and beyond all you can **hope**, ask, or think (Ephesians 3:20) (emphasis added).

In Luke chapter 5 we see an account of Jesus coming to His disciples after they had fished all night and caught nothing. He told them to go out into deeper water and lower their nets again. When they did something amazing happened.

> And when they had done this, they caught a great number of fish; and as their nets were [at the point of] breaking,
> They signaled to their partners in the other boat to come and take hold with them. And they came and filled both the boats, so that they began to sink.
>
> Luke 5:6–7

Consider the Source

Quite often when things don't work out, we get bad advice, or are disappointed by a friend, someone might say to us, "Well, what did you expect, considering the source." In other words, they are saying what we put our confidence in was shaky and we were bound to get hurt.

One of the reasons more people aren't overflowing with hope is because they're putting their hope in the wrong things. They're relying on a job, a relationship, the economy, a political ideology, a dream, or even a spouse to make them happy and fulfill their needs rather than looking to God. There is nothing wrong with any of those things at first glance, but they were never meant to be the very source of your hope. God is the only source that never runs dry. We talked in the beginning of the book about the importance of our hope having God as its source, but it is so easy for us to drift away from this important truth that I wanted to include it again in this final chapter.

1 Corinthians 8:6 says:

> Yet for us there is [only] one God, the Father, Who is the Source of all things and for Whom we [have life], and one

Lord, Jesus Christ, through and by Whom are all things and through and by Whom we [ourselves exist].

God is the "Source of all things" and He is the One in "Whom we have life." If your hope is based on anything other than God, you're going to be disappointed. The emotional stress many believers live under happens because they're relying on the wrong sources. If your hope is in a person, in a program, or even in yourself, you're going to suffer frustration and heartache time and time again because these are limited sources. And the longer you try to draw from these dry wells, the deeper and more pronounced the disappointment will be.

Psalm 42:11 says, "Why are you cast down, O my inner self? And why should you moan over me and be disquieted within me? **Hope in God** and wait expectantly for Him, for I shall yet praise Him, Who is the help of my countenance, and my God" (emphasis added).

David was doing something really wise in this verse of Scripture. Even though He felt downcast, and even though he didn't necessarily feel hopeful, he started talking himself into putting his hope in God. He told himself *I will hope in God today, and I will praise Him. It doesn't matter whether I feel like it or not. God is my source, and I will put my hope in Him!* He ignored his mood and decided to hope in the only Source who could sustain him. David had experienced the delivering power of God in the past, and he knew that God is faithful.

I could not begin to count the number of times that God has shown His faithfulness in my life, and you probably can say the same thing. Why should we waste our time depending on something shaky? Let's put our hope in the right source and avoid lots of disappointment.

What Hope Looks Like

Niagara Falls is one of the most awesome and breathtaking sights in all of North America. Even if you haven't been there to see it for yourself, you've undoubtedly witnessed its majesty on television or in pictures. The mighty rush of the river and the deafening crash of the waterfall are truly awe-inspiring. The wonder and beauty of the world God created never ceases to amaze me!

I think one of the most fascinating things about Niagara Falls is the fact that the falls never run dry. More than 6 million cubic feet of water pour over the falls every minute,[1] and this is never-ending. There is never a day when the Niagara River stops running and the park rangers send everyone home so they can restock the water supply. Minute after minute, hour after hour, day after day, the water continues to flow.

If you've visited Niagara Falls, you know you can't go anywhere near it without being affected. As you're walking up through the park, even before you see it, you can hear it. The sound of cascading water on the rocks below is extremely loud. And when you do get close, you start to feel the mist. The spray of the waterfall hangs in the air, and anyone who is anywhere near this natural beauty ends up drenched. It's a never-ending wonder that impacts every person who comes in contact with it.

This paints a great picture of what hope can be in your life. Just like a river that has never run dry, hope continues to flow. You can swim in it, drink it, share it with others—no matter how many times you draw from it, you can't exhaust it. Proverbs 23:18 promises that "your hope and expectation shall not be cut off." That means there will never be a time when you go to the river of hope and find a dry riverbed. Because God is eternal, hope in Him springs eternal. Every day of your life, you can go to Him, full of faith and hope, trusting that He is going to provide what you need.

Not only is hope a river that never runs dry, hope is a waterfall that affects everyone who comes near it. You can hear it, see it, and feel it in the air around you. When you are overflowing with hope, it not only impacts your life, it impacts all those around you. Your hope spills out onto them. The more they come into contact with you, the more they hear the roar of the waterfall and feel the mist in the air. Before long, they're saying "I just like being around you. There's something different about you. I feel hopeful when I talk to you."

When you get up each morning, believing God for something good to happen in your life, think of the waterfall. Anytime you're tempted to get discouraged and give up on a dream God has put in your heart, think of the waterfall. And anytime there are people around you who need encouragement, think of the waterfall. Hope isn't a trickle. Hope isn't a stream. Hope is a mighty, rushing waterfall that people will travel the world to come and experience.

What Are You Going to Believe?

A critical and cynical world will constantly warn you not to get your hopes up. It will tell you, "Things didn't work out in the past," or "Don't set yourself up for disappointment." You may be urged to be "reasonable" and not expect too much, but God tells us to expect more than what would be reasonable. He wants us to expect *more* than enough!

I want to encourage you to do just the opposite of what the world would do. Don't let your carnal mind rule your life. Renew your mind according to God's Word and learn to think as God does. In every chapter of this book, we've seen Scriptures and promises from God encouraging you to hope for His best in your life. We've seen biblical examples. We have heard the stories of ordinary people like you and me—men and women who dared to hope that God would fulfill His promises. The question must be asked: Which choice will you make? Will you choose hope or hopelessness? Are you ready to live with a happy anticipation that something good is happening today in you, through you, for you, for your family, in your children, in the world, to your friends, in your circumstances, at your workplace, at school, in the government, et cetera? One thing is for sure: Hopelessness and negativity will never improve anything, but if there is any possibility that hope and faith in God does work, then why would we not want to try it?

One of the boldest lies the enemy will tell you to keep you from living in the power of hope is that you don't deserve it. *You don't deserve to ask God for more. You don't deserve to believe for His best. You don't deserve to enjoy your life, because you've made too many mistakes along the way.* The world, the flesh, and the devil will remind you of your flaws and your failures, your sins and your shortcomings, and condemnation will try to keep you from approaching God with a hopeful heart.

The truth is this: You don't deserve hope...and neither do I. We've both messed up too many times; and if hope was dependent on our own righteousness, we'd fall way short of earning it. But the power of the Gospel is that when God sees us, He doesn't look at our failed attempts at righteousness; instead, He sees the perfect work of Jesus' righteousness. When we were still in the midst of our sins, broken and far from God, Jesus came and paid the price for us. His death paid for every sin, every mistake, every failure, and every shortcoming. There was no way we could earn anything God has given us, but God knew that, so He didn't ask us to. We've been given hope, not because we paid for it, but because Jesus did. And His payment was more than enough.

> We've been given hope, not because we paid for it, but because Jesus did. And His payment was more than enough.

Hope Brings...

A release of pressure
A positive change in your mood
A release from depression
The desire to dream again
A promise of better days ahead

A softening of a hard heart
A refreshed spirit
Motivation to reach your goals
Energy to your soul
Calmness to your mind and emotions
Freedom from worry
Freedom from fear
Enjoyment of life
Patience while you're waiting
Confidence that prevents you from giving up
The belief that anything and anyone can change
A reminder that God is in control
Excitement about the unknown
Confidence that it is never too late to begin again
The realization that you are not alone

This is only a small part of what hope brings, but to be honest, even if you lived with hope and none of these things happened, hope is still worth having because you will be happier with it than you ever could be without it!

Go Ahead and Get Your Hopes Up!

There is no limit or restriction on hope. The more you believe, the more pleased God is. But remember—hope is only as strong as its source. If your hope is in a person, a job, or your own strength and ability, you'll find yourself unhappy and frustrated. All of those things have limitations, but God does not—let Him be the source of your hope. Go through the day singing a hymn written in 1834 by Edward Mote.

My hope is built on nothing less
Than Jesus Christ, my righteousness;

I dare not trust the sweetest frame,
But wholly lean on Jesus' name.

On Christ, the solid Rock, I stand;
All other ground is sinking sand,
All other ground is sinking sand.

When darkness veils His lovely face,
I rest on His unchanging grace;
In every high and stormy gale,
My anchor holds within the veil.

His oath, His covenant, His blood,
Support me in the whelming flood;
When all around my soul gives way,
He then is all my hope and stay.

When He shall come with trumpet sound,
Oh, may I then in Him be found;
In Him, my righteousness, alone,
Faultless to stand before the throne.[2]

Go ahead and get your hopes up! There is no reason not to. Join the millions of others who have stepped out onto hope over the centuries and have never been sorry they did!

AFTERWORD

We began the first chapter of this book talking about Bad-News Betty. Poor Betty—she was a mess, wasn't she? Though she had a great family, and though she really loved the Lord, she had very little hope. Betty didn't have a happy anticipation that good things were going to happen; she had a discouraged anticipation that bad things were inevitable. Instead of assuming the best, Betty braced for the worst... and it was affecting her life.

Frustrated, worried, downcast, or discouraged, maybe you can relate to Betty on some days. Maybe you've struggled at times to really experience the abundant, overcoming, joy-filled life Jesus died to give you. Maybe you bought this book because the title sounded like good news, and good news was something you desperately needed.

Well, before I send this manuscript to the publisher, I want to take a moment to speak to you on a personal level. You see, I have high hopes for you. I believe God is going to free you from the heavy chains of "I can't" and "It's too late," so you can soar on the wings of "I can" and "The time is just right." I have a happy anticipation that you're going to leave the discouragement and despair of your past where it belongs—in your past—and you're going to run into the promise of your future.

I don't know exactly what you're going through as you read these words. Things might be going great, and you could be excited about a new adventure or opportunity. Or perhaps you're barely getting by, settling for "good enough" and thinking *It couldn't get much worse.*

Or it's possible you're hurting so deeply that you wonder if the pain will ever go away.

Whatever challenge you're facing today—no matter how big or small—it's time to hope again. It's time to hope for favor. It's time to hope for breakthrough. It's time to hope for happiness. The obstacle before you is an opportunity for God to do something amazing in your life. You're not going to lose—God is on your side, and God's undefeated.

So get up and get going. Raise your level of expectation. Refuse to settle for "good" when you've been promised "great." Today is a new day in your life—and a new day is a perfect time to get your hopes up.

NOTES

Chapter 1: Raise Your Level of Expectation

1. Source unknown; "Where's the Pony" http://storiesforpreaching.com /category/sermonillustrations/hope/.

Chapter 2: Follow the Leader

1. James Brown, Evangeline Baptist Church, Wildsville, LA, in *Discoveries*, Vol. 2, No. 4 (Fall 1991).

Chapter 3: Identify and Eliminate Every "Can't"

1. "About us," "I Have a Dream Foundation," http://www.ihaveadream foundation.org/html/history.htm; http://www.sermonillustrations .com/a-z/h/hope.htm.
2. *Today in the Word*, MBI, December 18, 1991.

Chapter 4: The Energy of Hope

1. Cited in Joyce Meyer, "Doing Your Best with What You Have," http://www.joycemeyer.org/articles/ea.aspx?article=doing_your _best_with_what_you_have.

Chapter 9: Keep Moving

1. Debra S. Larson, "Blind Skier Sets Goals on Disabled Olympics," February 5, 1987, http://articles.latimes.com/1987-02-05/news /vw-1122_1_water-skiing.

Chapter 10: Look for the Good in Everything

1. Source unknown, "Attitude," http://www.sermonillustrations.com /a-z/a/attitude.htm.
2. Source unknown, "Hope," http://www.sermonillustrations.com/a-z/h /hope.htm.

Chapter 11: Prisoners of Hope

1. *Bits & Pieces*, July 1991.

Chapter 12: Be an Answer to Someone's Prayer

1. Gary Morsch and Dean Nelson, *The Power of Serving Others: You Can Start Where You Are* (San Francisco: Barrett-Koehler Publishers, Inc., 2006), 19–21.
2. Cited in *Today in the Word*, March 6, 1991.

Chapter 14: Don't Wait For Tomorrow

1. "Misery Dinner," Christopher News Notes, August 1993, http://www.sermonsearch.com/sermon-illustrations/1185/misery-dinner/.

Chapter 16: The Choice Is Yours

1. The Capuchin Franciscans "Fasten Your Seat Belts," http://www.beafriar.com/New%20Projects%202012/Our%20Father%20is%20the%20Pilot.pdf.
2. Steve Goodier, *Quote* magazine, in *Reader's Digest*, May 1990.

Chapter 17: Let Hope Overflow

1. Niagara Parks, "Niagara Falls Geology Facts & Figures," http://www.niagaraparks.com/about-niagara-falls/geology-facts-figures.html.
2. "My Hope Is Built on Nothing Less," http://www.hymnal.net/en/hymn/h/298#ixzz31E5ASKsi.

ADDITIONAL BIBLE VERSES ABOUT HOPE

The pages of this book are filled with Scriptures about hope, but I've listed a few more below for additional encouragement.

Hope for Daily Living

The Lord is my portion or share, says my living being (my inner self); therefore will I hope in Him and wait expectantly for Him.

Lamentations 3:24

Rejoice and exult in hope; be steadfast and patient in suffering and tribulation; be constant in prayer.

Romans 12:12

Now faith is the assurance (the confirmation, the title deed) of the things [we] hope for, being the proof of things [we] do not see and the conviction of their reality [faith perceiving as real fact what is not revealed to the senses].

Hebrews 11:1

But in your hearts set Christ apart as holy [and acknowledge Him] as Lord. Always be ready to give a logical defense to anyone who asks you to account for the hope that is in you, but do it courteously and respectfully.

1 Peter 3:15

For with God nothing is ever impossible and no word from God shall be without power or impossible of fulfillment.

Luke 1:37

Behold, the Lord's eye is upon those who fear Him [who revere and worship Him with awe], who wait for Him and hope in His mercy and loving-kindness.

Psalm 33:18

O Israel, hope in the Lord! For with the Lord there is mercy and loving-kindness, and with Him is plenteous redemption.

Psalm 130:7

For whatever was thus written in former days was written for our instruction, that by [our steadfast and patient] endurance and the encouragement [drawn] from the Scriptures we might hold fast to and cherish hope.

Romans 15:4

Uphold me according to Your promise, that I may live; and let me not be put to shame in my hope!

Psalm 119:116

Let Your mercy and loving-kindness, O Lord, be upon us, in proportion to our waiting and hoping for You.

Psalm 33:22

Remember [fervently] the word and promise to Your servant, in which You have caused me to hope.

Psalm 119:49

By having the eyes of your heart flooded with light, so that you can know and understand the hope to which He has called you, and how rich is His glorious inheritance in the saints (His set-apart ones)...

Ephesians 1:18

This was so that, by two unchangeable things [His promise and His oath] in which it is impossible for God ever to prove false or deceive us, we who have fled [to Him] for refuge might have mighty indwelling strength and strong encouragement to grasp and hold fast the hope appointed for us and set before [us].

Hebrews 6:18

So shall you know skillful and godly Wisdom to be thus to your life; if you find it, then shall there be a future and a reward, and your hope and expectation shall not be cut off.

Proverbs 24:14

But this I recall and therefore have I hope and expectation: It is because of the Lord's mercy and loving-kindness that we are not consumed, because His [tender] compassions fail not.

Lamentations 3:21–22

My soul languishes and grows faint for Your salvation, but I hope in Your word.

Psalm 119:81

You are my hiding place and my shield; I hope in Your word.

Psalm 119:114

Those who reverently and worshipfully fear You will see me and be glad, because I have hoped in Your word and tarried for it.

Psalm 119:74

Through Him you believe in (adhere to, rely on) God, Who raised Him up from the dead and gave Him honor and glory, so that your faith and hope are [centered and rest] in God.

1 Peter 1:21

But we do [strongly and earnestly] desire for each of you to show the same diligence and sincerity [all the way through] in realizing and enjoying the full assurance and development of [your] hope until the end.

Hebrews 6:11

Now may our Lord Jesus Christ Himself and God our Father, Who loved us and gave us everlasting consolation and encouragement and well-founded hope through [His] grace (unmerited favor), comfort and encourage your hearts and strengthen them....

2 Thessalonians 2:16–17

Such hope never disappoints or deludes or shames us, for God's love has been poured out in our hearts through the Holy Spirit Who has been given to us.

Romans 5:5

I am hoping and waiting [eagerly] for Your salvation, O Lord, and I do Your commandments.

Psalm 119:166

With a view to this we toil and strive, [yes and] suffer reproach, because we have [fixed our] hope on the living God, Who is the Savior (Preserver, Maintainer, Deliverer) of all men, especially of those who believe (trust in, rely on, and adhere to Him).

1 Timothy 4:10

Hope for Salvation

Praised (honored, blessed) be the God and Father of our Lord Jesus Christ (the Messiah)! By His boundless mercy we have been born again to an ever-living hope through the resurrection of Jesus Christ from the dead.

1 Peter 1:3

[And He did it in order] that we might be justified by His grace (by His favor, wholly undeserved), [that we might be acknowledged and counted as conformed to the divine will in purpose, thought, and action], and that we might become heirs of eternal life according to [our] hope.

Titus 3:7

Awaiting and looking for the [fulfillment, the realization of our] blessed hope, even the glorious appearing of our great God and Savior Christ Jesus (the Messiah, the Anointed One)...

Titus 2:11–13

[Resting] in the hope of eternal life, [life] which the ever truthful God Who cannot deceive promised before the world or the ages of time began.

Titus 1:2

But we belong to the day; therefore, let us be sober and put on the breastplate (corslet) of faith and love and for a helmet the hope of salvation.

1 Thessalonians 5:8

Because of the hope [of experiencing what is] laid up (reserved and waiting) for you in heaven. Of this

*[hope] you heard in the past in the message of the truth of
the Gospel.*

Colossians 1:5

*If we who are [abiding] in Christ have hope only in this life
and that is all, then we are of all people most miserable and
to be pitied. But the fact is that Christ (the Messiah) has been
raised from the dead, and He became the firstfruits of those
who have fallen asleep [in death].*

1 Corinthians 15:19–20

JOYCE MEYER is one of the world's leading practical Bible teachers. Her daily broadcast, *Enjoying Everyday Life*, airs on hundreds of television networks and radio stations worldwide.

Joyce has written more than 100 inspirational books. Her bestsellers include *Power Thoughts*; *The Confident Woman*; *Look Great, Feel Great*; *Starting Your Day Right*; *Ending Your Day Right*; *The Everyday Life Bible*; *Approval Addiction*; *How to Hear from God*; *Beauty for Ashes*; and *Battlefield of the Mind*.

Joyce travels extensively, holding conferences throughout the year and speaking to thousands around the world.

JOYCE MEYER MINISTRIES U.S. & FOREIGN OFFICE ADDRESSES

Joyce Meyer Ministries
P.O. Box 655
Fenton, MO 63026
USA
(636) 349-0303

Joyce Meyer Ministries—Canada
P.O. Box 7700
Vancouver, BC V6B 4E2
Canada
(800) 868-1002

Joyce Meyer Ministries—Australia
Locked Bag 77
Mansfield Delivery Centre
Queensland 4122
Australia
(07) 3349 1200

Joyce Meyer Ministries—England
P.O. Box 1549
Windsor SL4 1GT
United Kingdom
01753 831102

Joyce Meyer Ministries—South Africa
P.O. Box 5
Cape Town 8000
South Africa
(27) 21-701-1056

OTHER BOOKS BY JOYCE MEYER

21 Ways to Finding Peace and Happiness

100 Ways to Simplify Your Life

Any Minute

Approval Addiction

*The Approval Fix**

*Battlefield of the Mind** (over three million copies sold)

Beauty for Ashes

*Change Your Words, Change Your Life**

*The Confident Mom**

The Confident Woman

*Do Yourself a Favor…Forgive**

*Eat the Cookie…Buy the Shoes**

The Everyday Life Bible

*Get Your Hopes Up!**

*Good Health, Good Life**

I Dare You

*Living Beyond Your Feelings**

*Living Courageously**

Look Great, Feel Great

*The Love Revolution**

*Making Good Habits, Breaking Bad Habits**

Never Give Up!

The Penny

*Perfect Love (Previously published as God Is Not Mad at You) **

*Power Thoughts**

The Power of Simple Prayer

Start Your New Life Today

The Secret Power of Speaking God's Word

The Secret to True Happiness

*You Can Begin Again**

Devotionals

Battlefield of the Mind Devotional

The Confident Woman Devotional

*Ending Your Day Right**

Hearing from God Each Morning

Love Out Loud

New Day, New You

The Power of Being Thankful

Power Thoughts Devotional

*Starting Your Day Right**

Trusting God Day By Day

**Also available in Spanish*